Enneagram

Visible Learning and Deep Learning Book for Highly Sensitive Person

Anita Anne Lambert

E

E

This page intentionally left blank

ℰ

Table of contents

E

Introduction

The Enneagram is a system of nine personality which has spread to many countries around the world for applications in family life, psychotherapy, spiritual direction, education, and business. The success of Enneagram is due to its practicality. Describing nine different type of personalities with their own point of views, Enneagram structure simplified a complex psychological system creating a map of different personalities that can be useful for people in their daily lives. By understanding each particularities of Enneagram personalities type, people can increase their self-awareness and their skill in communication and relationships of all kinds. Through knowing our habits of thinking, feeling and behaving we can access the talents and intelligence of our personality rather than simply being controlled by it. The first two chapters present a vision of the functionality of human brain while the following ones aims at investigating what make us stand among other people. Knowing your strengths and weakness through Enneagram you can reach your full potential. Later, it will be explained different ways of learning and the helpful method of concept maps which make you remember things easily and in a proper way. The next chapter is focused on how sensitivity allows you to identify the resources and practices that support deep work on yourself. Knowing the defenses of your personality type is vital whether you are committed to your own growth and to becoming more present and caring in our relationships. Understanding your defenses, when and how they are activated, is one of the most valuable applications of the Enneagram. The final chapter shows you that Enneagram pinpoints three parts of our defenses: the idealization, what you think you should be or what you want to live up to; the avoidance, what you try to stay away from and the defense mechanism.

Chapter One

Human Brain

Without understanding the brain it would not be possible to know the different patterns of brain activities associated with expert performers compared with novices or how learning can be an effective response to the decline of aging, or why certain learning difficulties are apparent in particular students even when they seem to be coping well with other educational demands.

The human brain is approximately the size of two hands placed next to each other or that of a coconut. Its weigh is around 1.5 kg. Our brain is a bustling hub of electrical activities. This is due to the fact that the cells in our brain called neurons use electricity to communicate with each other.

Neurons remember the form of the leafless trees, multiple branches called dendrites, which are responsible for making connections with other neurons. Neurons pass their messages through axons and are covered with a substance called myelin that acts as an axon insulator.

The brain produces electrical waves which can not be seen but can be measured. A test called an EEG can identify and measure the electrical activity in your brain. With a series of small metal discs called electrodes all over your scalp. The discs convey the electrical activity of your neurons through wires to a machine, which records and prints the patterns out on a screen or paper.

Brain waves occurs when a group of neurons sends an electrical signal to another group of neurons. However, there are actually five common types of brain waves. Alpha brain waves are only one type of brain wave. Brain waves are measured by frequency, which is cycles per second, or hertz (Hz), and they range from very slow to very fast. Alpha waves fit in the middle of the spectrum, between theta waves and beta waves. From slowest to fastest you can find:

- Delta (0.5 and 4 Hz): When you're deep in a state of

dreamless sleep, your brain is producing delta waves, which are the slowest type of brainwave;

- Theta(4 and 8 Hz): When you're sleeping more lightly or when you are extremely relaxed, your brain may produce more these type of waves;

- Alpha (8 and 12 Hz) which fall in the middle of the brain wave spectrum. Brain produces these waves when we are not focusing too hard on anything in particular. Whatever you're doing, you're probably feeling relatively calm and relaxed;

- Beta (higher-speed beta waves, 12 and 35 Hz): when you are going about your activities of daily living and making decisions so when you are wide awake, alert, and focused;

- Gamma (upward of 35 Hz): when your brain produces the speediest of brain waves, when for instance you are actively involved in processing information and learning. You're concentrating and

solving problems, and these brainwaves are the proof of your activities.

When your brain is producing these waves, it is responding to activities like meditation and rest that can reduce your stress levels and help you feel calmer. For instance, while you're warming up your muscles, your brain is producing alpha waves. It implies that you are in a state of wakeful rest. In other words, if you are able to produce alpha brain waves, that can help you get some rest and relaxation.

In a 2015 study, researchers found evidence that they could trigger a surge in creativity if they specifically focused on enhancing alpha waves. In fact boosting your alpha waves might also increase your creativity levels. In another study 20 participants were asked to participate in a randomized trial where to rev up their brain's production of alpha brain waves it was use the noninvasive brain stimulation.

Can alpha waves be interrupted ?

If for some reason your brain isn't producing very many alpha waves, it means that you're not in a relaxed, meditative state of mind but it goes without saying that your brain does not stop producing one type of brain wave just because you shift into a different state of consciousness or alertness. It is more that one type of brain wave will dominate at any given time, based on whether you're awake or asleep, focused, or floating along.

However there are times when your brain waves can become imbalanced. Some research pointed out that some people who have depression may have an imbalance of alpha waves, with more of them occurring in an area of the brain called the left frontal cortex.

Transcranial alternating current stimulation (tACS) is a brain stimulation technique that could increase alpha brain waves and reduce depression symptoms in people affected by major depressive disorder MDD.

Whatever you are doing there is always some type of electrical activity going on in your brain even if you are not aware of it. When your brain's alpha waves are dominating, you're likely in a state of wakeful relaxation. At different times of the day, depending on what you're doing, one type of your brain's electrical waves will dominate.

Relaxation techniques like mindfulness and meditation may help increase your alpha waves, and as a consequence, help you feel calmer, less anxious and may even boost your creativity levels.

Right and left part of the brain

Every time you learn something, myelin preserves the neuron and the neuronal area, making permanent what you have just learned. This preservation process is called myelination and it is considered the triple cycle of learning skills. The first part of the cycle is a general or global vision in which ideas desires and so are predicted.

The second part refers to the relationship and elaboration of the information so is the part where concepts are refined, as well as where a complementary analytical process is performed.

In the third part the data are transferred to everyday life to all areas of human existence. Synapses is the place where two nerve cells interconnect and other nerve terminals memorization is achieved.

The brain is divided into two equal parts: righ and left t cerebral hemisphere.

The left cerebral hemisphere, which joins each other through the corpus callosum, is made up of 200 million nerve fibers. The whole processes combines parts to integrate the random learning, rhythms, images and imagination, colors, dreams, recognition of faces, patterns, maps and dimensions. Not to mention intuition, creative capacity.

On the other hand, the left part of the brain is more and processes analytical performances which are more logical and has to do with reasoning, numbers, linear thinking and analysis.

Brain can also be divided into other three parts:

- Reptile brain which is responsible for maintaining the safety of the person. It is the cause of responses such as very informative, territoriality, rituals, disappointment.

- Cortical brain or Neomamiferous brain performs long-term planning, and solves problems, has to do with language, composition, and translation, creativity of art, music and theater.

- Limbic or Mammalian brain is responsible for providing daily needs, feelings of joy or sadness, energy and motivation. It is also responsible for social ties, hormones, sexual feelings, emotions, long-term memory.
When the limbic system detects the priority of a situation there is a release of chemical substances that create a kind of interference, blocking rational functions and not allowing us to think logically, be creative. All you can do is

being alert. In such occasion the heart may dominate reason.

Historically Limbic system was called the "emotional brain". Evidence show us that accumulating our emotions actually re-sculpt neural tissue. Some stress is essential to meet challenges and can lead to better cognition and learning, but beyond a certain level it has the opposite effect. In fact, in situations of excessive stress or intense fear, social judgment and cognitive performance suffer through compromise to the neural processes of emotional regulation.

Different stimulus

Every information we receive reach the cerebral cortex of our listeners, and it will be classified as interesting, important or accompanied by intense emotion. There are three types of memory: Fleeting memory, which lasts only a few moments; Working memory that keeps enough data present to perform a job, and Permanent memory that allows us to remember in the long term.

However, in large of the time our memory is influenced by our emotional state: If we are nor in the mood of doing something or we are "under the weather" we tend not to forget easily.

Stress can classified into the Distres and Eustres:

- Distres means that the stimulus we receive is negative producing reactions in the mammalian brain;

- Eustres is when the stimulus is positive and means that having a goal makes us acting more efficiently.

The Pygmalion effect

The phenomenon of the Pygmalion effect owes its name to the protagonist of a myth in ancient Greece related to Ovid in his "Metamorphosis." In this myth, Pygmalion is the king of Cyprus and a very skilled sculptor who spends his whole life looking for the perfect woman to turn her into his wife, but he does not succeed. Pygmalion think the perfect women does not exist, so he decide to sculpture a beautiful ivory woman free of imperfections. His projects followed all his desires and personal tastes sooner transforming the sculpture into a reflection of the creator. Once the statue was taking shape, the sculptor fell in love with the woman, whom he called Galatea. Pygmalion prayed to the gods to grant him a woman similar to the one sculpted in ivory. His wish come true. When he kissed the statue it came alive: a woman who in turn also falls in love with Pygmalion.

The theory is based on the principle that what is expected by one person can influence the behavior of another.

As a consequence our paradigms or beliefs can either stimulate or discourage results, motivation and quality of productivity. The expectations of the leader will influence the results of his or her subordinates based on how he leaded treated them. If subordinates are treated well their level of productivity will increase. In addition, your expectations will influence your way of treating other people and your way of treating them will influence the results.

Just as the Pygmalion effect refers to the way that other

people's expectations of us affect our performance, the Galatea effect refers to the way our expectations change us. That is to say, if a person feels capable and sure of themselves, they will surely have more possibilities of reaching their goals since they will direct their behavior towards those objectives without hesitations.

Beside Pygmalion effect there is also Galatea effect. It happens when you feel incapable and insecure. Due to doubts it will be much easier for you to focus on your failures, making your commitment to these goals more fragile.

These two phenomena have a straightforward relationship between them since the expectations that others have can significantly influence the way we feel about our abilities.

These theory explains how four factors are essential to obtain an optimization of results:

- Climate or all nonverbal messages from the leader. The climate can communicate both negative and positive expectations.

- Feedback, can be of greater or of lesser degree according to what the leader expects from the employee;

- Amount of data or information. - What the leader provides to the subordinate;

- Performance or lack of performance is influence by the leader's behavior.

By this it means that behaviors are imitated and an influence is reflected in all members and to achieve better results there must be harmony. It goes without saying that the way in which you try to approach a person may influence his or her reaction.

The way we respond to others members behaviors can not be taken for granted. There must be harmony in order to achieve better results.

The Golem Effect

Johann Wolfgang Goethe, a German poet and dramatist believed that if we treat a person as what he is, he will remain what he is; but, if we treat it as what it could be, then it will become all that it can become.

The Golem effect is a psychological phenomenon in which lower expectations placed upon individuals lead to poorer performance by the individual. In school, students who end up labeled as "bad students" or "less intelligent" receive less attention, and actually end up losing motivation and doubting their abilities. The interesting thing about this is that we can see how the concept of "being" is blurred. As a human being we are not "static" or permanent, but we keep changing and evolving to interact with their environment. Educators have a role that can be vital in compensating for socioeconomic differences among students, and are able to reinforce more those that can have added difficulties to reach their maximum potential.

Both the Golem Effect and the Pygmalion Effect demonstrate the power of the self-fulfilling prophecy. They show that people tend to both live up to expectations and that expectations tend to influence the judgment of behavior and output, Golem for negative expectations, Pygmalion for the positive. The tragedy is that certain marginalized groups who are the most vulnerable. The danger of low expectations can be insidious. Stereotypes of a race to differentially-abled to the elderly to the mentally ill and addicted. Create a cycle that, if not monitored, perpetuate itself.

The first tool we have is awareness. For the individual being under observation, it is vital to be aware of one's talents, strengths, retain self-awareness, seek mentoring, and create multiple streams of feedback. Endeavor to promote positive feedback and place the emphasis on solutions while demonstrating strategies for development and success. For leaders, it is imperative to attempt to view the individual in a clear manner and to encourage and evaluate in an honest and fair way.

E 19

Chapter Two

SWOT Analysis

A SWOT analysis is a high-level strategic planning model that helps organizations identify where they're doing well and where they can improve, both from an internal and external perspective. It is an acronym for *"Strengths, Weaknesses, Opportunities, and Threats."* This analysis provides advice on how students can use their learning modalities and skills to their advantage when studying for an upcoming test or assignment. Generally it is preferable to conduct a SWOT analysis at the beginning of your strategic planning process or during a strategy refresh.

The exact origin of SWOT Analysis has been debated. Some people believe that it originated in the 1950s at Harvard Business School and was the work of professors George

Albert Smith Jr and Kenneth Andrews. Others believe it was created by Albert S. Humphrey in the 1960s during his time at the Stanford Research Institute.

Let's see more in details the SWOT strategies:

- Visual SWOT Strategies utilize graphic organizers such as charts, graphs, and diagrams for redraw your pages from memory. Otherwise, symbols or initials in order to replace important words as well as colors to highlight important key terms;

- Aural SWOT Strategies which record your summarized notes and listen to them on tape. After having a discussion with others you have to expand upon your understanding of a topic. Other strategies make you read loud your notes and/or assignment and explain your notes to your peers/fellow "aural" learners;

- Read/Write SWOT strategies consist of write and rewrite your words and notes. The idea behind that is to gain a deeper understanding. Doing so you may also organize diagrams, charts, and graphic organizers into statements;

- Kinesthetic SWOT Strategies utilize real life examples, applications and case studies in your summary to help with abstract concepts using pictures and photographs that illustrate your idea.

Other applications of SWOT Analysis

SWOT analysis has become very popular, and may be one of the most widely used management decision-making tools among business managers. Your entire leadership team should be heavily involved, because they should have the ability to look across your organization and offer insight into your competitive environment and/or business landscape. When the leadership team offers appropriate recommendations regarding your strengths, weaknesses, opportunities, and threats, you will end up with a SWOT analysis that has the credibility to be used constructively in the strategic planning process. The ultimate goal of SWOT analysis is to achieve a more successful outcome; for a company, the goal may be to improve performance and enhance growth.

SWOT analysis can hypothetically be used by any type of organization as a decision-making tool. It can also be used by individuals for similar purposes. One of the most appealing feature of SWOT analysis is its universal applicability. Consider the following examples:

- EdTech designers: When a project is created, SWOT analysis can identify factors that lead to the eventual success of the project, while also considering risks and areas that need improvement;

- Small and medium companies use SWOT analysis to formulate, implement and evaluate strategies that may lead to improvements in productivity, performance, and successful operation of the company;

- Farming and agricultural development. According to some researchers the use of SWOT Analysis is useful and precious in the context of farming and agricultural development as happened in Iran;

- Private schools. SWOT analysis was used in an attempt to improve two different private schools. The researchers stated that the analysis benefited one of the schools by allowing it to "advance in the face of growing challenges thereby leading to its stability and increased productivity"

- Nursing policy – Some researchers have used SWOT analysis to consider the nursing policies of multiple European countries. Their analysis allowed them to identify factors that prevented collaboration between countries.

SWOT Analysis can gather data about internal issues within a company or project, both strengths and weakness, and external issues outside of the company or project, opportunities and threats. It then analyzes this data to inform future goals, decisions, and strategies.

The visual learning style means that people need to see information to learn it, and this "seeing" takes many forms from spatial awareness, photographic memory, color/tone, brightness/contrast, and other visual information. Naturally, a classroom is a very good place for a visual learner to learn. Teachers use overheads, the chalkboard, pictures, graphs, maps, and many other visual items to entice a visual learner into knowledge.

The importance of environment

It has been recognized that the close interdependence of physical and intellectual well-being are remarkably connected. By treating our minds and bodies correctly, it is possible to take advantage of the brain's potential for plasticity and to facilitate the learning process.

Nurturing is also crucial to the learning process, and are beginning to provide indication of appropriate learning environments. Many of the environmental factors conducive to improved brain functioning are the quality of social environment and interactions, nutrition, physical exercise, and sleep, which may seem too obvious but most of the time easily overlooked. The brain responds very well to this: Concerning positive emotions, one of most powerful triggers that motivates people to learn is the illumination that comes with the grasp of new concepts.

A primary goal of early education should be to ensure that children have this experience of "enlightenment" as early as possible and become aware of just how pleasurable learning can be.

One of the key skills of being an effective learner managing one's emotions. Neuroscience, drawing on cognitive psychology and child development research, starts to identify critical brain regions whose activity and development are directly related to self-control. Self-regulation is one of the most important behavioral and emotional skills that children and older people need in their social environments.

Why do we need to learn?

Every time that you try something new you change. You change by learning. Learning is of vital importance because learning is changing, and changing is growing. Especially when it comes to new ideas knowledge, skills, and behavio The formula of growing is:

"Ambition + discipline + learning= growing"

You gain experience with what you have learned by applying it in your everyday situation. Keeping learning is necessary because what you know is not static and you constantly need to catch up with your abilities in order to avoid aging. An essential competence for learning is the technique of learning itself. Graduates have learned a lot, but rarely how to learn. They know the theory learn through school books. Learning is not devouring all books. That helps, but it is not enough.

Learning takes time and money. Learning is working 'on' your company. Not only people but also many organizations do not take time to update and learn something new. Without a defined learning strategy and a budget there is not a structure.

Scaling up is about learning. Let take entrepreneurs as an example. They need to growth mindset. Its is unquestionable. With the right growth mindset, you are ready to improve yourself.

Learning provides a mountain of information about how you can do it differently without wasting time. Learning is a process, and you need to apply it in an organization. A learning organization is more than adding up all personal development plans.

Decide what the organization should change and what employees must learn for that. Look for the best trainers, coaches, courses, and conferences. Let employees reflect on what they learn and how they will performance it.

Organizing a monthly meeting in which an employee tells

what he or she has learned recently is a quite simple but extremely inspiring strategies for the audience. Explaining in front of an audience who one has learned is a concrete help to master one knowledge.

The Pygmalion effect it is aso known as the self-fulfilling prophecy or Rosenthal effect. Rosenthal was a professor of social psychology at Harvard University who, together with Leonore Jacobson, the school director, initiated a famous experiment to demonstrate the effects of the self-fulfilling prophecy in education. They gave a non-verbal intelligence test to the students at the beginning of the course, informing the teachers that the analysis predicted the intellectual capacity of the students. Then, they randomly selected a sample of 20% of the students in each class, thus creating the experimental group. Selected students seemed to have more significant potential for progress, while the rest did not say anything, the latter becoming the control group.

After eight months, an intelligence test was passed on to all the students, showing a significant improvement in the experimental group compared to the control group. They generate a better climate and are more open to giving information and feedback. Also giving more opportunities and presenting higher challenges offer the selected students more resources to develop their skills, since they start from a more stable base. Those students who had been rated as more capable had improved more than the rest.

In conclusion, the above experiment allowed scientists to demonstrate that the positive expectations of those around us have a direct effect on our performance and our results.

Regardless of the method or variant used, when you need to learn something new there are common factors that everyone uses: relaxation exercises, visualization induction, suggestions (pygmymeon effect), special music adapts to the type of learning, breathing exercises to help brain synchrony and decrease stress.

The ability to learn is the capacity that every human being has but not everyone has been encouraged to exploit ones capabilities. Saying that we can develop our own skills it may sound a bit odd but it is true because. Typically we tend not to push too hard since carrying out these techniques is somewhat complicated and requires a lot of discipline.

Since kindergarten it would be better to teach more learning techniques in schools as subjects because this would help to improve performance in all areas of a person. If you stop practicing your abilities eventually these that can disappear. To achieve proper thinking, both brains are required to work simultaneously. The different techniques that stimulate the right brain can be the difference between success and failure. In particular, some techniques might stimulate throughout the right hemisphere including visual thinking, fantasy, evocative language, metaphors, direct laboratory experimentation, travel, simulation and multi-sensory learning.

Plasticity

According to neuroscientists, plasticity is a process that happens to the brain because it has a highly robust and well-developed capacity to change in response to environmental demands. Plasticity is a core feature of the brain throughout life. The degree of modification depends on the type of learning that takes place, with long-term learning leading to more profound modification. This involves creating and strengthening some neuronal connections and weakening or eliminating others. It also depends on the period of learning, for example babies experiencing extraordinary ability to memorize. There are optimal or "sensitive periods" during which particular types of learning are most effective, despite this lifetime plasticity.

There are relatively tight and early sensitive periods where sensory stimuli such as speech sounds, certain emotional and cognitive experiences such as language exposure. Other skills, such as vocabulary acquisition, do not pass through tight sensitive periods and can be learned equally well at any time over the lifespan. Adolescence is an extremely important period in terms of emotional development partly due to a surge of hormones in the brain. Nowadays adolescent brain is far from mature, and undergoes extensive structural changes well past puberty. This is due to the fact that the still under-developed pre-frontal cortex among teenagers may be one explanation for their unstable behavior. "High horsepower, poor steering" is the exact combination of emotional immaturity and high cognitive potential.

On the contrary, in older adults, fluency or experience with a task can reduce brain activity levels. Most studies have shown that learning can be an effective way to counteract the reduced functioning of the brain: whether through adult education, work or social activities, the more there are opportunities for older and elderly people to continue learning, the higher the chances of deferring the onset or delaying the acceleration of neurodegenerative diseases.

Math mind

From the fact that brain structures are designed through evolution for language, there are analogous structures for the quantitative sense. And, also as with language, genetically-defined brain structures alone cannot support mathematics as they need to be co-ordinated with those supplementary neural circuits not specifically destined for this task but shaped by experience to do so.

However, numeracy and the brain Numeracy, like literacy, is created in the brain through the synergy of biology and experience. Whether in schools, at home, or in play, Neuroscience is opening new avenues of identification and intervention. In this sense the role of education play an important role.

Understanding the underlying developmental pathways to mathematics from a brain perspective can help shape the design of teaching strategies. Although the neuroscientific research on numeracy is still processing, the field has already made significant progress in the past decade. It shows that the mere representation of numbers involves a complex circuit that brings together sense of magnitude, and visual and verbal representations. Calculation calls on other complex distributed networks, varying according to the operation in question: subtraction is critically dependent on the inferior parietal circuit. Even very simple numerical operations are distributed in different parts of the brain and require the co-ordination of multiple structures. Research on advanced mathematics is currently sparse, but it seems that it calls on at least partially distinct circuitry. Different instructional methods lead to the creation of neural pathways that vary in effectiveness. Drill learning, for instance, develops neural pathways that are less effective than those developed through strategy learning. Support is growing from neuroscience for teaching strategies which involve learning in rich detail rather than the identification of correct/incorrect responses.

Mathematics requires the full functioning and integrity of specific brain structures. Dyscalculia, the numerical equivalent of dyslexia, are still under-researched, the discovery of biological characteristics associated with specific mathematics impairments suggests that mathematics is far from a purely cultural construction. It is likely that the deficient neural circuitry underlying dyscalculia can be addressed through targeted intervention because of the "plasticity"or the flexibility of the neural circuitries involved in mathematics.

Over the past few years, there has been a growing number of misconceptions circulating about the brain. These neuromyths are often have their origins in some element of sound science, which makes identifying and refuting them the more difficult. They are relevant to education as many have been developed as ideas about how we learn. As they are incomplete, extrapolated beyond the evidence, or plain false, they need to be dispelled in order to prevent education running into a series of dead-ends.

The importance and promise of this new field are not the reason to duck fundamental ethical questions which now arise. Each "myth" or set of myths is discussed in terms of how they have emerged into popular discourse, and of why they are not sustained by neuroscientific evidence as follows:

- "There is no time to lose as everything important about the brain is decided by the age of three."

- "There are critical periods when certain matters must be taught and learnt."

- "But I read somewhere that we only use 10% of our brain anyway."

- "I'm a left-brain and she's a right-brain person."

- "Let's face it ! Men and boys just have different brains from women and girls."

- "A young child"s brain can only manage to learn one language at a time."

- "Improve your memory!"

- "Learn while you sleep!"

Language ability

The brain is biologically primed to acquire language right from the very start of life. There is an inverse relationship between age and the effectiveness of learning many aspects of language. Neuroscience has started to identify how the brain processes language differently among young children compared with more mature people. Generally, the younger the age of exposure, the more successful the learning. This understanding is relevant to education policies especially regarding foreign language instruction which often does not begin until adolescence.

The process of language acquisition needs the catalyst of experience. Adolescents and adults can also learn a language from the scratch, but it presents greater difficulties.

Much of the brain circuitry involved in reading is shared across languages but there are some differences, where

ℰ 37

specific aspects of a language call on distinct functions, such as different decoding or word recognition strategies. Understanding how phonetics and semantic processes are at work argues for a balanced approach to literacy instruction that might target more phonetics or more "whole language" learning, depending on the morphology of the language concerned.

Within alphabetical languages, the main difference discussed in this report is the importance of the "depth" orthography of a language. A language is "deep" when maps sounds onto letters with a wide range of variability such as English or French contrasts with "shallow", much more "consistent" languages such as Finnish or Turkish. In these cases, particular brain structures get brought into play to support aspects of reading which are distinctive to these particular languages.

Atypical cortical features which have been localized in the left hemisphere in regions to the rear of the brain are commonly associated with dyslexia which results in impairment in processing the sound elements of language. The linguistic consequences of these difficulties are relatively minor (e.g. confusing words which sound alike), while impairment can be much more significant for literacy as mapping phonetic sounds to orthographic symbols is the crux of reading in alphabetic languages.

Everyone is unique

Everyone is created differently and equally. This notion of individualized learning styles has gained widespread recognition in education theory and classroom management strategy. The term "learning styles" refers to the ability of every person to learn differently. An individual's learning style takes into consideration the preferential way in which the person absorbs, processes, comprehends and retains information. For example, when learning how to build a clock, some students focused their attention to the process by following verbal instructions, while others physically manipulate the clock themselves. Individual learning styles depend on one's prior experience or background and on cognitive, emotional and environmental factors. In other words everyone's different. It is important to understand the differences in one's learning styles, so that they can implement best practice strategies into daily activities, and in case of students, curriculum and assessments. This is the reason why most degree programs, specifically higher level ones such as doctorate of education, integrate different learning styles and educational obstacles directly into program curriculum.

Understanding VARK

The learning styles are found within educational theorist Neil Fleming's VARK model of Student Learning which is an acronym that refers to the four types of learning styles: Visual, Auditory, Reading/Writing Preference, and Kinesthetic. The VARK model is also referred to as the VAK model, eliminating Reading/Writing as a category of preferential learning.

One of the most accepted understandings of learning styles is that learning styles fall into three main categories: Visual Learners, Auditory Learners and Kinesthetic Learners. The

VARK model recognizes that students have different approaches to how they process information, referred to as "preferred learning modes." By understanding what kind of learner you and/or your students are, you can now gain a better perspective on how to implement these learning styles into your lesson plans and study techniques. The main ideas of VARK are outlined in Learning Styles Again:

- Individual' preferred learning modes have significant influence on their behavior and learning.

- Individual' preferred learning modes should be matched with appropriate learning strategies.

- Information that is accessed through modality preferences shows an increase in their levels of comprehension, motivation, and metacognition.

- Allowing individual to access information in terms they are comfortable with will increase their academic confidence. Identifying people as visual, auditory, reading/writing or kinesthetic learners, and aligning your overall curriculum with these learning styles, will prove to be beneficial for your way of learning things and in classroom.

Learning styles

Learning styles and preferences take on a variety of forms and not everyone fit neatly into one category as there's plenty of overlap between styles. In general most learners align with the following styles:

- Auditory learners person who tend to learn better when the subject matter is reinforced by sound. These individuals would much rather listen to a lecture than read written notes, and they often use their own voices to reinforce new concepts and ideas. This type of people like to read out loud to themselves and are great at verbally explaining things and also they aren't afraid to speak up in public and. Watching videos and using music or audiotapes are also helpful ways to engage with auditory learners. They are the first to invoke group discussions so their auditory and verbal processors can properly take in and understand the information they're being presented with;

- Kinesthetic learners or "tactile" learners acquire information through experiencing or doing things. These individual might be good at sports or like to dance, need to take breaks when studying and might not have great handwriting so they like to get right in the thick of things by acting out events or using their hands to touch and handle in order to understand concepts. The best way to discover them is by getting them moving. Once these people can physically sense what they're studying, abstract ideas and difficult concepts will be easier to understand;

- Reading/ writing learners are learners who prefer to learn through written words. These types of learners are drawn to expression through writing, reading articles on the internet, writing in diaries, looking up words in the dictionary and searching the internet for just about everything. Allow plenty of time for these learners to absorb information through the written word, and give them opportunities to get their words out on paper as well. This is probably the easiest learning style to cater to since most of the educational system provides lots of opportunities for writing essays, doing research online and reading books;

- Solitary learners are those individuals who are self-motivated and highly independent so they do prefer to learn on their own. They favor a quiet environment both in their personal and academic lives. If you need to sit alone and study by yourself in order to retain information you are a solitary learner. Other activities includes: Privilege self-analysis; dislike large crowds and noisy rooms; write a journal, diary or record personal thoughts and events as a way to improve; Set goals and make plans;

- Naturalistic learners: like kinesthetic learners, they are more in tune with nature. They use elements and patterns in the natural world to create products and solve problems. They can categorize and catalog information easily and have a preference for exploring outdoors. They tend to dislike learning unfamiliar topics with no connection to nature but have a strong interested in subjects, such as biology, botany, and zoology. For example, people who prefers reading in a hammock or on a swing to a stuffy classroom and loves digging in the dirt is most probably a naturalistic learner.

- Visual learner are individuals with a preference for visual learning is partial to seeing and observing things, including pictures, diagrams, written directions and more. Learners who learn through sight understand information better when it's presented in a visual way. It is also referred to as the "spatial" learning style. These are your doodling students, your list makers and your students who take notes. They always need to create opportunities to draw pictures and diagrams on the board, or ask students to doodle examples based on the topic they're learning. Visual learners should regularly make handouts and use presentations. They may need more time to process material, as they observe the visual cues before them.

By equipping learners with tools in their early years, they will be equipping for their futures. Pinpointing how a child learns best can dramatically affect their ability to connect with the topics you're teaching, as well as how they participate with the rest of the class.

As the name suggests this learning style requires the learners to first see what they're expected to know. They may also need to map out their thoughts in order to process them better. These are some of the most common characteristics of visual learners:

- Have good spatial awareness and sense of direction;
- Can easily visualize objects, plans, and outcomes;
- Like coloring, drawing, and doodling;
- Have good color balance;
- Are good at using maps and rarely get lost.

For example, a visual learner in a writing class may process the information better by seeing a movie clip of how a film adapts the literature it was based on, instead of listening to the book being read aloud.

Chapter Three

Myers-Briggs Type Indicator (MBTI)

According to an investigation carried out in 2004 by researchers Saville and Holdsworth Enneagram could be comparable to other well-known and more accepted theories including the Myers-Briggs Type Indicator (MBTI) and the Big Five.

Classifying what makes people who they are has been a challenge in the world of personality psychology. To better understand aspect of human personality **a** lot of theories and models have been developed over years. Trait psychology insists on the idea that people differ from one another in terms of where they stand on a set of basic trait dimensions that persist over time and across situations. Personality traits reflect people's characteristic patterns of thoughts, feelings, and behaviors.

Big Five Personality Traits

Numerous studies have attempted to find links between personality traits and brain morphometry, but most have relied on relatively small samples and have not yielded consistent and replicable findings. Importantly, a recent study has suggested that even samples of 300 participants may be too small to reliably detect associations between psychological phenotypes and brain morphometry. This lack of statistical power has been further compounded by varied methodological and analytic approaches across studies.

Understand and classifying what makes people who they are has been a longstanding challenge in the world of personality psychology. The Big Five personality traits or five factors model (FFM), is a widely examined theory of five broad dimensions used by some psychologists to describe the human personality.

The Big Five personality traits are considered to be broad and global factors that can be further partitioned to a set of hierarchically lower-order facets, reflecting narrower, yet intercorrelated, sub-components of each broad dimension. However, despite the statistical consistency of the Big Five personality traits, uncovering the biological mechanisms that underlie them has been challenging. Each of these Big Five personality traits create a pair of opposites which were used to assess the Big Five personality dimensions and their underlying facets:

1. Neuroticism (based on the anxiety, angry hostility, depression, self-consciousness, impulsiveness, and vulnerability facets); It is sometimes called emotional instability, or in reversed it is referred to as emotional stability. Neuroticism is the tendency to experience negative emotions, such as anger, anxiety, or depression. A high need for stability manifests as a stable and calm personality but can be seen as uninspiring and unconcerned. A low need for stability causes a reactive and excitable personality, often very dynamic individuals, but they can be perceived as unstable or insecure.

2. Agreeableness (based on the trust, straightforwardness, altruism, compliance, modesty, and tender-mindedness facets) Agreeableness trait reflects individual differences in general concern for social harmony. They are generally considerate, kind, generous, trusting and trustworthy, helpful, and willing to compromise their interests with others while high agreeableness is often seen as inexperienced or obedient. They are inclined to value harmony more than they value their own say. Contrary, low agreeableness personalities are often competitive or challenging people, which can be seen as aggressive or untrustworthy. They focus more on their own needs than the needs of others.

3. Conscientiousness (based on the competence, order, dutifulness, achievement striving, self-discipline and deliberation facets) is a tendency to show self-discipline, act dutifully, and aim for achievement against measures or outside expectations. It is related

to the way in which people control, regulate, and direct their impulses. High conscientiousness is often perceived as stubborn and obsessive while low conscientiousness is flexible and spontaneous but can be perceived as sloppy and unreliable;

4. Extraversion (based on the warmth, gregariousness, assertiveness, activity, excitement-Seeking, and positive emotions facets); reflects a person's comfort level with relationships. Extroverts are characterized by excitability, sociability, talkativeness, assertiveness and high amounts of emotional expressiveness. Oppositely, introverts are less sociable, less talkative, less assertive, and more reluctant to begin a new relationship;

5. Openness-to-Experience (based on the fantasy, aesthetics, feelings, actions, ideas, and values facets) addresses one's range of interests. Extremely open people are fascinated by novelty and innovation. It is a general appreciation for art, emotion, adventure,

unusual ideas, imagination, curiosity, and variety of experience. People who are high in this trait tend to be more adventurous and creative while people low in this trait are often much more traditional and may struggle with abstract thinking.

Big five personality traits were the model to comprehend the relationship between personality and organizational behaviors and modern researchers began by studying known personality traits and then factor-analyzing hundreds of measures of these traits in order to find the underlying factors of personality. The potential value of this framework lies in the fact that it encompasses an integrated set of traits that appear to be valid predictors of certain behaviors in certain situations.

MBTI

In the 1920s, based on the classical work of Carl Jung the Swiss Psychiatrist, the Myers-Briggs Type indicator ask people how they usually feel or act in particular situations.

Based on the answers received, people are differentiated in terms of four general dimensions: sensing, intuiting, judging and perceiving. He felt that although people had all four of these dimensions in common, they differ in the combination of their preferences of each. Whereas the Big-Five has recently emerged from considerable basic research and has generally been demonstrated to significantly relate to job performance, the MBTI is based on a very old theory, has mixed at best research support, but is widely used and very popular in real-world career counseling, team building, conflict management, and analyzing management styles. Myers-Briggs is the most prevalent personality test used by British businesses to expose the inner personalities of employees. Its success, many claim, lies in its simplicity.

The MBTI is a very popular instrument used to assess personality types. It is widely used in the selection process. As many as two million people are reported to be taking it each year in the U.S.A.; research suggests that the MBTI is a very useful method for determining communication styles and interaction preferences. The essence of the MBTI theory is that much seemingly random variation in the behavior is actually quite orderly and consistent, being due to basic differences in the ways individuals prefer to use their perception and judgment.

Judgment involves all the ways of coming to conclusions about what has been perceived. Perception involves all the ways of becoming aware of things, people, ideas happenings around us. If people differ systematically in what they perceive and in how they reach conclusions, then it is only reasonable for them to differ correspondingly in their interests, reactions, values, motivations, and skills.

The aim of the developer was to make the insights of type theory accessible to individuals and groups. Two related goals in the developments and application of the MBTI instrument were identified:

1. The identification of basic preferences of each of the four dichotomies specified or implicit in Jung's theory;

2. The identification and description of the 16 distinctive personality types that result from the interactions among the preferences.

Sixteen Primary Traits

Here there are 16 distinct types of personality traits.

1. Reserved Vs. Outgoing.

2. Less intelligent Vs. More intelligent.

3. Affected by feelings Vs. Emotional more stable.

4. Submissive Vs. Dominant.

5. Serious Vs. Happy-go-lucky.

6. Expedient Vs. Conscientious.

7. Timid Vs. Venturesome.

8. Tough-minded Vs. Sensitive.

9. Trusting Vs. Suspicious.

10. Practical Vs. Imaginative.

11. Forthright Vs. Shrewd.

12. Self-assured Vs. Apprehensive.

13. Conservative Vs. Experimenting.

14. Group dependent Vs. Self-dependent.

15. Uncontrolled Vs. Controlled.

16. Relaxed Vs. Tense.

How Personality Traits Influencing Organizational Behaviors

- Self-Monitoring: refers to the extent to which a person is capable of monitoring his or her actions and appearance in social situations. A personality trait that has recently received increased attention is called self-monitoring. High social monitors are sensitive to the types of behaviors the social environment expects from them. They can modify their behavior according to the demands of the situation and to manage their impressions effectively is a great advantage for them. Generally, they are rated as higher performers, and emerge as leaders. They also tend to be more successful in their careers. They are more likely to get cross-company promotions, and even when they stay with one company, they are more likely to advance;

- Self-Efficacy: is a belief that one can perform a

specific task successfully. Whatever you do this is a good predictor of whether we can actually do it. Self-efficacy at work is related to job performance. The relationship is probably a result of people with high self-efficacy setting higher goals for themselves and being more committed to these goals, whereas people with low self-efficacy tend to procrastinate. Giving people chances to test their skills so that they can see what they are capable of doing is also a good way of increasing self-efficacy. This means that hiring people who are capable of performing their tasks and training people to increase their self-efficacy may be effective;

- Proactive Personality: refers to a person's inclination to fix what is perceived as wrong, change the status quo, and use initiative to solve any type of problems. Eager to learn and with the desire to engage in many developmental activities to improve their skills, they adjust to their new jobs or tasks quickly because they understand the political environment better and often make friends more quickly. Proactive people are valuable assets to their companies because they may have higher levels of performance becasuse, instead of waiting to be told what to do, proactive people take action to initiate meaningful change and remove the obstacles they face along the way;

- Self-Esteem: is the degree to which a person has overall positive feelings about his or herself. They are in general confident, and respect themselves. High self-esteem is related to higher levels of satisfaction with one's job and higher levels of performance on the job. Contrarily, people with low self-esteem experience high levels of self-doubt and question their self-worth;

- Locus of Control: refers to the degree to which people feel accountable for their own behaviors. People with a high internal locus of control believe that they control what happens to them is their own doing, while those with a high external locus of control feel that things happen to them because of other people, luck, or a powerful being. The people who believe that they control their destinies have been labeled internals, whereas the latter, who see their lives as being controlled by outside forces, have been called externals. It is possible that externals may see less of a connection between how they live and their health while internals takes more responsibility for their health and adopt healthier habits, while. Successful entrepreneurs tend to have high levels of internal locus of control;

- Risk-Taking: refers to the people willingness to take chances, how an individual is willing to take chances and make risky decisions. For example high-risk taking managers make more rapid decisions and useless information in making choices in comparison with low risk-taking managers. Managers in large organizations, tend to be risk-averse, especially in contrast to growth-oriented entrepreneurs who actively manage small businesses. Their propensity to assume or avoid risk has been shown to have an impact on how long it takes managers to make a decision and how much information they require before making their choice;

- Positive and Negative Affectivity: Are people that tend to be in a good mood most of the time and regardless of what is actually going on in their lives they feel like others are in a bad mood most of the time. This distinction is manifested by positive and negative affectivity traits. Positive affective people tend to be happier all the time and their happiness spreads to the rest of the work environment so teams dominated by positive affective people experience lower levels of absenteeism and more inclination to collaboration. In addition positive affective people experience positive moods more frequently, while negative affective people experience negative moods with greater frequency;

- Type A Personality:describes an individual who lives at a higher stress level as ambitious, rigidly organized, highly status conscious, can be sensitive, care for other people, are truthful, impatient, take on more than they can handle, want other people to get to the point, proactive, and obsessed with time management. They enjoy the achievement of goals, with greater enjoyment in achieving of more difficult goals. They hate failure and will work hard to avoid it. They are generally pretty fit and often well-educated. They find it difficult to stop, even when they have achieved goals. They are thus constantly working hard to achieve these;

- Type B Personality:is in contrast to those with Type A personalities. They are often reflective, thinking about the outer and inner worlds. They live at a lower stress level and typically work steadily, enjoying achievements but not becoming stressed when they are not achieved. They work steadily, enjoying achievements but not becoming stressed when they are not achieved. When faced with competition, they do not mind losing rather they enjoy the game. They never suffer from'a sense of time urgency with its accompanying impatience. Very creative people who enjoy exploring ideas and concepts. They are often reflective, thinking about the outer and inner worlds. They play for fun and relaxation, rather than to exhibit their superiority at any cost;

- Machiavellianism: take its roofs to Niccolo Machiavelli, a sixteenth-century author that explained how the nobility could more easily gain and use power. Machiavellianism is now used to describe behavior directed at gaining power and controlling the behavior of others. Research suggests that Machiavellianism is a personality trait that varies from person to person. Generally, high Machs manipulate more, win more, are persuaded less, and persuade others more than do low Machs. Yet these high Mach outcomes are moderated by situational factors when they interact face to face with others rather than indirectly. Otherwise, when the situation has a minimum number of rules and regulations, it allows freedom for creativeness, and when emotional involvement with details irrelevant to winning distracts low Machs;

• Motivation: understand what motivates a person is quite hard. The way of motivating the persons should be understood. People can be motivated solely by money with the promise of bonus or compensations. Other people prefer recognition among their peers, so celebrating their successes at a staff luncheon or sending out a recognition email to the staff could keep those employees working at full steam. Other are self-motivated, able to work hard for the personal satisfaction they receive when they achieve the goal;

- Work Ethic: develops in people who make their jobs a high priority. People with a weak work ethic often require more management and oversight to keep them focused on their work or task, whereas people with a strong work ethic typically work well with minimum oversight.

Chapter Four

Self-confident in learning

You can create conditions to build self-esteem and self-confidence. Self-esteem is formed by two components: the intellectual and the emotional, and it is really an attitude about oneself, a kind of attitude fundamental to the learning process.

How can you achieve self-confidence? There are 10 components to take into consideration:

1. High personal Integrity. The art of telling always the truth;
2. Responsibility: Be the cause of your action;
3. The support of others: Establish a win-to-win relationship;

4. Self-discipline: Everytime you set a goal, achieve it.

5. Build relationships: Make them last in the long term;

6. Know yourself: Your skills and your hidden ability;

7. Vision and purpose: Have goals of what you want to do in life;

8. Environment: Create an environment that allow you to grow and that reflects your greatest thoughts about yourself.

9. Excellence: Trying always your best;

10. Health: Take care of your body as well as your emotions and mental health.

Self-esteem and self-confidence are attitudes about ourselves, and these attitudes are fundamental for the learning process and we can encourage this process with some motivator such as music or positive message. There are three learning areas: Cognitive (what we know); Psychomotor (what we do) and Affective (what we feel).

Dealing with the use of positive suggestion, we can manage to motivate people intrinsically and foster self-confidence.

The presence of images, sounds, signs with motivating statements, use pleasant aromas should be contemplated.

There are no learner without resources: Self-esteem and self-confidence is a matter of attitude that nobody can impose on you and that cannot be built directly, but if we can create conditions for them to increase Since we have our intellectual and emotional side, we should feel able to make and solve any challenge or goal that we face and have a positive attitude towards life.

- Personal atmosphere;
- Area around us;
- Physical changes.

They tell us about how to explore an environment rich positive thinking, sense of security, relaxation, as well as curiosity and enjoy the activities that are carried out.
Available resources are:

- Personal skills;
- Learning techniques;
- Methodology

Use of multiple techniques that make learning a different and enjoyable experience such as: games (measure to repeat the information without boring), simulators (that the situation seems very real, can be very intense and leave traces and profound changes, metaphors, visualization, interaction. Visualization is done with closed eyes and music, guided by a person, whose voice must be according to the music, which takes us to any part of the universe, using all our senses.

Mind Maps: A Tool To Learn

Mind mapping is a highly effective way of getting information in and out of your brain..Human brain is a super computer but we barely know how it works. We need to know how harness is his power. Mind mapping is a creative and logical means of note-taking and note-making that literally "maps out" your ideas With mind maps we should understand how the brain get processes information. It is interesting to see that even the most complicated and long issues and concepts are easier to simplify, retain and capture, understanding their use.

All Mind Maps have some things in common. They can be defineted as a natural organizational structure that radiates from the center and use lines, symbols, words, color and images according to simple, brain-friendly concepts. The system converts a long list of monotonous information into a colorful, memorable and highly organized diagram that works in line with your brain's natural way of doing things. Special images or shapes can represent landmarks of interest or particularly relevant ideas.

There are many mind mapping software programs that may help you organize your thoughts and then automatically export them to an easy-to-read, ordered list. This kind of maps ca be compared to an external mirror of your own radiant or natural thinking facilitated by a powerful graphic process, which provides the universal key to unlock the dynamic potential of the brain.

Mind mapping works as a map of a city: The city center represents the main idea; the main roads leading from the center represent the key thoughts in your thinking process; the secondary roads or branches represent your secondary thoughts, and so on.

As soon as new idea pop into your head you are not constrained by thinking in order. Without thinking too much you simply throw out any and all ideas.

The Five Essential Characteristics of Mind Mapping are:

1. The main idea, subject or focus is crystallized in a central image;

2. The main themes radiate from the central image as 'branches';

3. The branches comprise a key image or key word drawn or printed on its associated line;

4. Topics of lesser importance are represented as 'twigs' of the relevant branch;

5. The branches form a connected nodal structure.

When you try to create a mind mapping you should think of your general main theme and write that down in the center of the page. Then figure out sub-themes of your main concept and draw branches to them from the center, It will begin to look like a spider web. Obviously, make sure to use very short phrases or even single words and to add images to invoke thought or get the message across better

There should be at least two main points for each sub-theme you created and create branches out to those.

This method is simpler than you think. You should use tools to free yout potential brain:

- The traditional linear form; Chronology words;
- Symbols;
- The drawings; the personal expression of an idea;
- The colors for integral communication.

Through mind mapping we can realize the way we control and develop the learning process more clearly. Mental maps are an important part of our university life, it is helpful to develop intelligence through thinking, since it requires constant ideas to make learning easier and thus take better advantage of the way of seeing things and life. It is required efficient memory style, quick reviews, deep study, focus on concepts, and ability to make concrete what is already learned in a more valuable way.

Through intellectual freedom everyone with passion for discovery can raise the standards of intellectual skills. Our brain is the only organ capable of studying itself, with good nutrition and training it can ever work more than a hundred years without being affected its power. Its full capacity is still unknown.

It is said that the conscious part of the mind is only 5 to 10% and that we have an extraordinary potential of information, memories, emotions inexpressive. The mind perceives by context, pictures, and scenes in such a way that when we focus our attention on the core issue we are recording all other data, emotions and sensations to a lesser extent. This is because of each existential experience the brain calcifies the messages and only what it considers important sends it to the intern. Our intelligence can be fostered, indeed our mind is able to learn and develop on its own merit, without age limitations, levels or traditional obstacles created by society.

Each one has a specific task but at the same time everything is interrelated allowing a very sophisticated way of handling thoughts, emotions and instincts.

For this reason every piece of information that enters the brain (codes, colors, flavors, textures or images) can be represented as a sphere from which several hooks start. Each of them represents an association which ahve infinite types of channels or loops.

The quadrants of the Suggested Methodology for Teaching Intelligence are four and are classified as following:

1. Sensitize: using the five 5 senses;
2. Teach: using 5 senses and emphasizing their relationship with the others;
3. Resize: Educating, activating, and deepening its potential;
4. Practice: costance is a key to achieve real-life growth.

Learning Strategies through Reflection

There are different ways to make learning visible during reflection. The most essential to help learners see their thinking and learning are those that help learners to view themselves as their own teacher, in other words responsible for their own efforts and learning.

- Think now: This is a prompt that you can discuss or write about. Use it halfway through any lesson or tasks that you have to do. Frequently pause and think about this prompt: prepare a list that will help you to see how their thinking is changing as a result of their work. Imagine key concepts that will be required in the task and then make a short checklist of those concepts. At the beginning of a lesson/tasks, ask yourself three ideas/facts you know and the analogy or connection you can make. At the end of the learning repeat again the same activity. You will realize that learning by writing one sentence to summarize how your efforts created learning. Write the learning in your own words. It might change a bit from what you intended. You can use this to bridge the gap between real expectations and the actual result;

- Self-Evaluation: As much as possible use a rubric or a scale. The best scales reveal what the learning looks like in specific actions and concepts. During and after learning tasks, try to evaluate your own learning. Ask

you briefly why they evaluate their own learning at that level. It's a simple strategy, but its impact is immense. Then ask what you may need to take it to the next level on the scale. You are not doing work, just to "get a grade". You are working toward a learning target. This is more than simply posting an objective. Could you imagine a track athlete going to practice each day, but not knowing what race they will run? Understanding what you need to understand better is the first step;

- The Grit Reflection: The key is learning, not work. It goes without saying that make connections is essential this means that in any task create a strategy is extremely powerful because it to make you learn links from one day to the next. This is used at the end of a learning task to boost confidence and resiliency. On a scale of 1-10, how much effort did you put forth? What strategies did you use? How has this helped you to be a stronger learner? What challenges did you face? What parts of the learning were hard for you? Where did you get stuck?

- The Extension Reflection: Visible learning includes raising student awareness of motivation and emotional engagement.

Individualistic contrasts

Self-observing intercessions encourage autonomous working, which enables people with inabilities to depend less on prompts from others. Self-observing mediation are among the most adaptable, helpful, and successful procedures for understudies with scholastic and conduct challenges. They have shown adequacy for focusing on a scope of scholastic capacities, self-improvement abilities conduct issues, and social practices Students with conduct and scholarly challenges ordinarily have restricted mindfulness and comprehension of their conduct and its impacts on others. Self-checking is helpful from preschool to adulthood and to people at an assortment of levels of psychological working. Self-checking techniques are individualized plans used to expand autonomous working in scholarly, conduct, self-improvement, and social territories. Self-checking mediations prepare understudies to perceive and monitor their very own conduct. Using these procedures, it can be figured out how to distinguish and expand positive, genius social practices, the practices important for achievement when all is said in done training settings. Contrarily to concentrating on lessening an understudy's undesired conduct, self-checking methodologies create abilities that lead to an expansion in proper conduct. At the point that self-checking abilities increase, comparing decreases in undesired practices frequently happen, even without direct intercession. This conduct change enables instructors and guardians to address various practices with one productive intercession. Five stages engaged with arranging a self-checking intercession have been discovered:

1. Identify objective conduct;
2. Select/plan a self-observing framework;
3. Choose reinforcers;
4. Teach the understudy to utilize the framework;
5. Fade the job of the grown-up in the mediation.

Chapter Five

What is Visual Learning Style?

As mention in the previous chapter Visual Learning is just one of the three different learning styles popularized by Neil D. Fleming in his VAK model of learning. The visual learning style means that people need to *see* information to learn it, and this "seeing" takes many forms from spatial awareness, photographic memory, color/tone, brightness/contrast, and other visual information. If you are one of those people who bring up mental imagery when you're trying to remember what you did last Tuesday afternoon, or you remember the cover of every book you've ever read or remember the exact location of where you left your car keys, you are probably one of those people with the visual learning style.

Naturally, a classroom is a very good place for a visual learner to learn. Teachers use overheads, the chalkboard, pictures, graphs, maps, and many other visual items to entice a visual learner into knowledge.

Visual learning at school

Visual learners typically do well in a modern classroom setting where there are whiteboards, handouts, photos, and so on. These students have many strengths that can boost their performances in school. Here are just a few of the strengths of this learning type:

- Easily visualizes objects;

- Notices minute similarities and differences between objects and people easily;

- Instinctively follows directions and have an excellent organizer mindset;

- Has a great sense of balance and alignment;

- Strong sense of color, and is very color-oriented

- Can see the passage from a page in a book in his or her mind;

- Envision imagery easily.

If you are a visual learner, you may find these things helpful when sitting in class or studying for a test. Visual learners need things in front of them to help solidify them in their brains, so don't try to go it alone when listening to lectures or studying for your next midterm. Be sure to integrate these tips into your study routine:

- Take notes during lectures to capitalize on your learning style;

- Be sure to read the diagrams, maps, and other visuals that go along with text to help you remember it;

- Color-code your notes, vocabulary words, and textbook and make to-do lists in an agenda;

- Any noise will distract you so study alone because you need to see things to remember them and often,;

- Use outlines and concept maps to organize your notes.

Visual Learning Strategies for Teachers

I know that most teachers don't like using statistics because they feel like losing yourself in a sea of statistical jargon. Moreover if you are truly committed to evidence-based education, you must understand some fundamental facts about educational research.

Which are understanding how to judge a research to acknowledge what this research is truly telling you. A teacher has to know that students with the visual learning style make up about 65 percent of a class. These students will pay attention to your overhead slides, whiteboard, Smart board, PowerPoint presentations, handouts, graphs, and charts. They will usually take good notes and will appear to be paying attention during class. If you use a lot of verbal directions without visual cues, visual learners may get confused, as they prefer to have something in writing to refer to.

The following strategies are ideal for reaching those students with the visual learning type:

- Supplement verbal lectures with a handout, diagram, or other visuals and use a lot of colors into your presentations;

- Enhance your presentations use funny video or PowerPoint with images;

- Give written instructions and expectations;

- Not only your reading in class but also solitary reading time during lessons;

- Beside lectures vary your instructional assignments with group work, solitary work, pairs, circles so every learner is challenged;

- Show your students how to complete a task and how to make great fashcards with vocabulary and numbers;

- Provide written feedback on assignments.

There is no doubt that teachers can make a great difference in how well their students do at school. When you explore the thousands of research studies on the topic, it is clear that some teaching strategies have far more impact than others. The list of teaching strategies to make it on this list has to contain:

•Be supported by hard research, rather than anecdotal case studies or untested theories;

•Have an impact on student results that it is substantially higher than typical strategies;

•Utilize a wide range of subject areas and in all year levels.

Clear Lesson Goals

It is crucial that you are clear about what is the topic of your lesson and what you want your students learn during each lesson. Holding high expectations has a sizeable effect, anyway the effect that such clarity has on student results is 32% greater1 than the effect of holding high expectations for every student.

Lesson goals state what you want your students to: Know and understand and be able to do. Clear lesson goals would help you and your students to focus every other aspect of your lesson on what matters most.

The second core teaching strategy in this list is tell and show. It is a good idea yo start most of your lessons with some show and tell:

•Telling involves sharing information or knowledge with your students

•Showing involves modelling how to do something.

Your lesson goals make clear what you want your students to know and be able to do by the end of the lesson: resuts. Now, you need to tell them what they need to know and show them how to do the things you want them to be able to do. Avoid spending your entire lesson having the students listening to you. Rather it is crucial to focus your show and tell on things that matter most. To do this, have another look at your lesson goal.

Check for understanding with questions

Once you have told students what they need to know, you need to check their understanding before moving on asking random sampling and see all student response system. Random sampling involves asking a question, pausing and then randomly choosing a student to answer. The pause is to allow all students to think of their answer before answering.

Additionally, the random sampling can be as simple as names out of a hat. Other popular techniques include popsicle sticks in sand and an online name picker. If you use random sampling at any lessons, your students get used to having to have an answer ready in case you select their name. By asking a small number of questions about the content you have just shared and randomly selecting students to answer them, you can get a reasonable estimate of the class's understanding. Another option is to use some form of all student response system. These systems include graphic outlines which include things such as mind maps, flow-charts and Venn diagrams. These are helpful to students to: summarize what they have learned and understand the interrelationships between the aspects of what you have taught them. A fantastic way to finish off your lessons is to discuss a graphical summary at the end. You can then refer to it one more time at the end of your lesson. If the graphic summary graphic is accurate it doesn't seem to matter who makes the summary graphic, be it you or your students.

What are Concept mapping and why are they useful?

A specific type of graphic organiser is concept mapping which involves representing and organizing interrelated knowledge visually and hierarchically. Concept maps have 3 key parts. The first and two parts are: The concepts normally written within rectangles or ovals and the relationships between them represented by labelled arrows. Putting together, the concept-relationship-concept structure makes propositions, which simply form the third key part of concept maps and reflect the key understandings of the material.

If you show the concepts within rectangles and the relationships with labelled arrows. The propositions or key understandings that it shows are: Matter with different state; Solids form with a type of state and states include solids; Liquids, another type of state and states; and finally Gases which are the third form of state and states include gases Their propositions don't have to be extremelly or correct in term of grammar. Here is a more developed example of a concept map of the concepts related to the states of matter. However, diagrams are not concept maps when they do not explicitly show the relationships between concepts. For example forms like: Hard Life, Chains and Australian History. They should not be placed on the same hierarchical level.

Your students' minds will not store million of information randomly. Rather, they store them in organized schema. that allow students to see how different pieces of information fit together. This includes how new information fits with what students already know as well as various bits of new information fit together.

Plenty of research has shown that concept mapping has a positive impact on all levels of schooling. However, some different review of research, finding that concept mapping seem not to be helpful in Mathematics. However, most studies focused on students in Middle and Secondary school found that concept mapping is useful in both stem and non-stem subjects, as well as English, science and Humanities.

Make sure to opt for concept mapping that is an extraordinary way to do this.

How to make a Concept Map

You can make concept maps by hand or using a computer (or iPad or similar). In the first case the process often involves moving concepts around, which can then require a lot of rubbing out. If you want your students to make a complex concept map by hand, then I suggest a bit of creative thinking. For example, you could use small colored Post-it notes on a blank piece of A3 paper. You connect the separate post-it notes with hand-drawn arrows and relationships and once you are happy with your map, you can copy it into a notebook.

There is another possibility to make concept maps with software (or apps). You can do this manually, using a generic graphics program such as Adobe Illustrator, or use a program specifically designed for concept mapping such as Inspiration.

Before you start asking your students to make concept maps, the teacher should make some concept maps yourself. It will help you to :

- •Understand what concept maps are good for and what they are not

- •To give better feedback and assistance to your students.

There are steps you should consider when making a complete concept map like:

- •Identifying your focus;
- •Listing your key concepts;
- •Grouping your key concepts into hierarchical levels;
- •Linking your concepts

After deciding my focus, you simply list the relevant concepts. Next, you need to arrange your concepts into a basic hierarchy. Doing this method again and again you will become an expert and this practice is also important for students to retain the knowledge and skills that they have learned during your show and tell. Therefore, research also shows that students do better when you give them multiple opportunities to practice spread out over time. Another opportunity to check for understanding is to choose practice tasks related to your lesson goal. This opportunity includes:

- Re-explain things to the class or groups;
- Offer personalised feedback to individual students.

What you need to do is build opportunities to practice past material either as part of the lesson or stand-alone sessions by themselves. You can also benefit of concept mapping yourself to help you do things like getting your own head around a unit topic. Research shows us that clarity has great benefits and concept mapping is only one way to achieve it. Furthermore, research has shown that concept mapping has a more substantial impact on student learning when they are used to help students learn central ideas, rather than details and within and beyond your classroom. Your students might actively engage with the map.

You should not ask students to do something you haven't shown them how to do in class. This means that concept mapping has more impact on student results when students use it in class, and for homework and assignments.

When you have to teach a unit to your student try to use concept mapping.

1. First at all start with the first 4 hierarchical levels.

2. Ask students to use their prior knowledge to come up with a list of what those objects include.

3. Clarify and correct their ideas by including the fifth level of the hierarchy. Showing them the key relationships;

Every time you need to expande other concepts, such as planet or solar system. Make separate concept maps and do the same thing for additional concepts. Then only show them in the overarching map, to explain key relationships, and eventually, only the relevant parts. Student improve their learning when students study teacher-made concept maps. But there is a larger impact on their results when they engage with the maps. Such engagement can either take the form of making their own maps or fill in the blanks type maps. For instance, in first lesson on solar system, after showing them the first 5 hierarchical levels of you own map, you should ask them to complete the following by themselves. In a second moment ask them to do it for homework. The more you repeat this task over time, and more they will improve. Each time asking them to do more of it themselves. Eventually, They will learn how to make the map solely from scratch.

More details about Concept mapping

The research shows that it doesn't seem to matter how long you use concept maps for. It could be a 3-week unit or even a 10-week unit. Students can complete concept maps individually or in small groups. It is also tolerated cases where students use static, animated or interactive concept maps. What matters is identifying your focus it may sound critical as maps can quickly become unwieldy. Use questions to focus your map. For example "What are the key features of the solar system? Organize yourself creating a list of your initial concepts. Brainstorm a list of relevant concepts and refer to trusted sources when necessary. After that group your concepts into levels of a hierarchy. Since concept maps show hierarchical relationships you need to group your concepts into broad hierarchical levels. Next step consist of linking your concepts establishing linking relationships between concepts by joining them with labelled arrows. One of the last things to do is looking for ways to enhance your map. You could include additional but relevant concepts and you can add in specific examples of concepts. You can also create cross-links and reciprocal links. Finally rewiew your map and see if some improvement are necessary. On top of normal proofreading, this step involves checking the appropriateness of your hierarchical levels and the accuracy of propositions.

Provide Your Students With Feedback

Feedback focuses on what your student did and they are different to praise but they are essential in a classroom.

Giving feedback involves telling a student: How they have performed on a particular task, along with ways that they can improve. Feedback provides your students with a tangible understanding of what they did well where they are at, or their actual level, and how they can improve from now on.

According to John Hattie's view, any teachers who seriously want to boost their children's results should start by giving them regularly of feedback. Otherwise, if you want to learn more about giving feedback.

Of course, it will require a lot of time to put everything into practice because each student can learn is not as revolutionary as it sounds. It underpins the way we teach martial arts, swimming and dancing. It is also the central premise behind mastery learning, a technique that has the same effect on student results as socioeconomic status and other aspects of home life.

When you adopt mastery learning, you differentiate differently. You keep your learning goals the same but vary the time you give each child to succeed. Therefore, use this strategy whenever and however you can.

Do not underestimate the power of group work is. Even if productive group work is rare, as some students do all the work and all the learning, while others do very little at all. There are several reasons this can happen, but 2 of the main one are that some students are more: Eager than others and competent than others. In order to increase the productivity of your groups, you need to be selective about the tasks you assign to them. Individuate role that each group member plays in advance. In addition you should utilize the evidence-based teaching strategy of productive group work Only for asking groups to do tasks that all group members can do successfully and ensuring each group member personally responsible for one step in the task. For instance when teaching students to multiply a 2 digit number start by showing the class what to and telling them why each step is important. Next check for understanding. Doing so, get your students to complete some practice again, recheck for understanding after they have done so. Only when all students are starting to develop competence should you give them group work.

In the next step you should: place your students into groups of 3, as there are 3 steps involved in 2 digit (2 digit multiplication). After that have each group member to decide to choose a letter, A, B or C.

1. Student A: multiplies the top number by the digit in the ones column of the second number;

2. Student B:multiplies the top number by the digit in the tens column of the second number;

3. Student C: add the number of steps 1 and 2;

4. Repeat again change group member as long as you wish.

Not Just Content

Beside show and tell strategies which focus was on teaching content you can also increase how well your students do in any subject by explicitly teaching them how to use relevant learning strategies such as:

- Assign writing homeworks that teach them strategies such as making a plan and checking for transition words;

- Read you often teach strategies that will deepen their comprehension;

- Mathematics and related problem-solving strategies.

From assignments and studying, the strategies that will help your students perform better. In this case you need to:

•Tell students about the above strategies;

•Show them how to use them;

•Give them guided practice and feedback before asking them to use them independently.

Nurture Meta-Cognition

Many teachers often ask their students to use some strategies, for example making connections when reading and self-verbalizing when solving problems. Of course, such strategies are useful, but actually they are not encouraging students to use meta-cognition.

Meta-cognition involves thinking about your options, your choices and your results. And it has an even larger effect on student results than teaching them strategies. When using Meta-cognition, the right thinking is take into consideration what strategies they could use (options), what strategies they will use (choices) and how effective their choices were (results). Consequently continue use them or change their chosen strategies.

There are also some popular teaching strategies that do not have a large effect on student results. These include whole language, teaching test taking and discovery-based learning. However, it does not imply that they are not good but probably they can only be used within a single subject rather than to a class.

Chapter Six

The Spacing Principle

Having the tendency to teach one thing and move onto the next, and students do not have enough spaced practice to cement new things within their long-term memories. Massed practice is still far more prevalent than distributed practice. The amount of time students need to remember what you have taught them. The ideal length between practice sessions varies. The spacing principle that supports distributed practice also supports other learning activities. Students benefit from distributing their study of the same material. It is preferable giving students time to practice doing the things you have taught them to do in class. But there are different types of practice, and they are not all equally effective. These include massed practice and distributed practice.

Massed Practice

Let's make an example of massed practice. Image you are teaching a class how to find the volume of a rectangular prism. You would firstly show your students how to do it. Then you would have your students do it themselves at home together with a few practice questions. You often ask them to do quite a few practice problems to help your students cement the steps in their minds. In this type of lessons there is no because there is only a small gap between practice sessions: A weak form of distributed practice. Massed practice is still quite common in many classrooms even if it is not the most effective way of helping your students to learn.

Massed practice works best when performers are highly motivated and when they have limited time for training sessions.

Growth mindset

A growth mindset is a particular way of looking at intellectual and other abilities. People with a fixed mindset believe that you are born with particular abilities (e.g. intellectual, social, creative) and that you can't do much to change them. Contrarily, individuals with a growth mindset acknowledge that nature bestows some natural abilities. But they also believe that they can develop their abilities and that people's potential is always unknown. A growth mindset is simply a belief that you can develop your abilities. People with good academic abilities, musical talent and sporting prowess have a growth mindset and believe that they can develop the abilities they were born with as their potential is truly unknown. One of the most common example is a belief that you can develop your intellectual abilities. People with a growth mindset believe that the mind is like a muscle that can be strengthened with use. You can apply the same principle to other abilities, such as physical prowess, musical aptitude and emotional intelligence. On the other hand, people with a fixed mindset believe that they are born with certain abilities but they are unable to develop their abilities. It is believed that having a growth mindset has a positive impact on individuals' success at school or on working place. This impact is even larger for students who struggle or who have hard home lives. Researchers conclude that that kind of people are better equipped to manage the challenges and setbacks they experience along the way.

Students with Growth Mindset vs students with Fixed Mindsets

Research demonstrates that students with a growth mindset tend to outperform students with a fixed mindset. Here is a visual example, showing the different way students with a growth mindset and fixed mindset respond to challenges, setbacks and failures. A 2018 meta-analytic review of research showed that it had a moderate effect on students' academic success. By comparison, research shows that self-efficacy had a large impact on students' learning.   This research is about the impact that having a growth mindset vs fixed mindset. It is not on the success of teachers' efforts to nurture a growth mindset. National Study of Learning Mindset is one of the largest studies in this area. David Yeager and his team of other researchers, including Carol

Dweck found that a short online and easy to administer intervention could have a moderate impact on students' mindsets and involved. Key features of online training included:

- 2 × 30-minute online sessions;
- Learning about the mindsets;
- An initial assessment of students' existing mindsets;

Reflecting on and writing about the mindsets.:

- More than 12,000 Year 9 students from 65 different schools;
- Students completing 2 × 30 minute online courses a few weeks apart;
- Looking at changes in their mindsets as well as later changes in their achievement levels.

This result is similar to the result of a 2018 meta-analysis conducted by Brooke Macnamara and her colleagues. It too showed that mindset programs only had a small impact on students' learning. Although, it showed a slightly larger impact for struggling students. According to Macnamara's study students from low-SES homes benefited more from mindset programs Additionally, growth mindset programs were more effective when they involved explicitly subject about the growth mindset outside of normal lessons and reading material that explains the growth mindset and its benefits, as well as writing about what they have read (e.g. writing to explain it to someone else) and a short programs (1-2 sessions) were just as effective as longer ones.

Given the small amount of time and effort it takes to teach students about the growth mindset, it may be something worth doing. Teaching students about the growth mindset, fixed mindset and their differences has a small, but positive impact on students' future success at school and in their lifes. Having a growth mindset rather than a fixed mindset has a moderate impact on how well students do at school. This impact seems to be long-lasting. This is especially the case for students from low-SES homes and for struggling students.

Distributed Practice and Massed Practice according to researchers

For a long time, researchers about training circulation have primarily focused on the amount of rest that should be set aside between practices to create an environment that enhances optimal learning because of the essential role it plays in engine learning.

Research demonstrates that distributed practice has far more impact on individuals' learning than massed practice. Distributed practice involves students practicing something over several sessions spaced out over time. This is quite different to massed practice, where the practice occurs in one intensive block. This is why this form of practice is both an evidence-based and a high-impact teaching strategy. Massed practice not at all like distributive practice is described by longer work time or dynamic practice with shorter rest.

On average, people who have undertaken distributed practice achieved 15% higher than students who had only completed massed practice. A distributive practice shows a comparable measure of work time or dynamic practice crosswise over different sessions. Be that as it may, the length of every session is shorter contrasted with massed plan. Despite this, the session is reached out over a critical period to understand the training destinations. What teachers, practice pioneers, or physical specialists take into consideration is how practice circulation use the allotted time between and inside training sessions. The rule of massed practice in an equivalent measure of study will result in improved adapting just if it is performed in unmistakable shorter time lengths than a solitary broadened period. Then, learning for all individuals will result under circulated rehearses in any case their age, racial foundation, where they dwell or whether they or not went to school.

Checking on data after the first learning procedure as opposed to investigating following the first learning procedure has happened results in better learning. Rehearsing or investigating the data at the ideal time is fundamental in improving learning results, in fact rehearsing the movement or auditing data once will not yield critical results. In this way the significant advantage of dispersed practice over its partner is the dividing impact and it is better to use distributed practice to learn and comprehend things properly. Undergrads appraised the probability of review of individual words exhibited with the expectation of complimentary scholarly. Expectations were made utilizing a seven-point scale quickly following a thing's introduction in the rundown. To-be-appraised things incorporated those introduced 1 time just as things displayed twice in either a massed or appropriated way. Twice-introduced things were appraised as bound to be reviewed than things displayed once, and they were reviewed in that capacity. In any case, despite the fact that Massed practice things were made a decision about bound to be reviewed than Distributed practice things, they were most certainly not. The finding that Ss misconceived when they knew MP things proposes why handling might be less for massed than for circulated introductions. Results bolster the constriction of consideration speculation with respect to the dispersing impact in free review.

To best remediate scholarly inadequacies, teachers need to apply instructional changes that outcome in increasingly proficient understudy learning and recognize experimentally approved mediations as well as the present investigation analyzed the impact of massed and conveyed practice with an unequivocal planning intercession to assess the degree to which these changes lead to expanded math actuality familiarity on essential expansion issues. Forty-eight third-grade understudies were set into one of three gatherings with every one of the gatherings finishing four 1-min math unequivocal planning systems every day crosswise over

19days. Gathering one finished every one of the four 1-min timings without interruption; bunch two finished two consecutive 1-min timings toward the beginning of the day and two consecutive 1-min timings toward the evening, and gathering three finished one, 1-min autonomous planning multiple times conveyed over the day. Development bend demonstrating was utilized to check the advancement over the span of the investigation. Results proposed that understudies in the circulated practice conditions, both four times each day and two times each day, indicated altogether higher familiarity development rates than those rehearsing just once every day in a massed configuration. These outcomes show that joining circulated practice with unequivocal planning methods is a helpful adjustment that upgrades understudy learning without the expansion of additional instructional time when focusing on math reality familiarity.

According an investigation analyzed the degree to which a practice methodologies affected learning a verbal data or scholarly ability task for second-and fourth-grade understudies. One hundred and ninety understudies from eight second-and fourth-grade study halls took an interest in the examination. Homerooms were randomly distributed to the two practice conditions and all understudies took an interest in a 9-week coordinated learning framework intercession. The examination found that scholarly aptitude assignments are found out marginally more successfully in a massed than conveyed practice mode, however the thing that matters was not factually critical. Similarly understudies learned verbal data errands more viably in the massed practice mode, however the thing that matters was not measurably noteworthy. The contrasts between the two practice conditions were not as incredible on verbal data errands, be that as it may, and no factually huge contrasts were found. It was closed from this examination, because of the moderate impact estimate contrasts and the indistinguishable cost factor for joining the two sorts of training, that the utilization of massed practice would be progressively reasonable for scholarly aptitude undertakings.

Extra examinations, utilizing the quantity of exercise units finished, showing that having finished a more noteworthy number of math exercises positively affected the math test scores. These investigations recommend that a more grounded treatment or better adherence to the treatment could have caused a critical impact for massed practice in scholarly aptitude areas. Rehearsing is expected to give an increasingly strong establishment to this statement. Massed practice is progressively viable in the higher request verbal data region. Solid research surmising proposes the duration of dispersed practice for lower level undertakings, especially in the verbal data regions. Further research is expected to find factors that breaking point or refute the dividing impact. A distributive practice, then again, displays a comparable measure of work time or dynamic practice crosswise over different sessions.

Within these lessons you can gradually learn and comprehend what you are trying to gain an understanding of. Put simply, distributed practice lessons are broken down into smaller lessons. Rehearsing or investigating the data at the ideal time is fundamental in improving learning results. Just like how we were taught in our own school system growing up and now in university our professors break the lessons down into sections. This is how we gain the knowledge we have today.

Chapter Seven

Sensitivity definition

Sensitivity is the capacity to respond to changes in the environment as well as the degree of response of a receiver or instrument to an incoming signal or to a change in the incoming signal. High sensitivity can be defined as acute physical, mental, and emotional responses to external, both social and environmental, or internal, intra personal stimuli. Some of the positive aspects of being a sensitive person such as greater ability to listen and affirm, greater empathy and intuitiveness, better understanding of others' wants and needs. A highly sensitive person may be an introvert, an extrovert, or somewhere in between.

Three are the most important Sensitivity: Sensitivity About Oneself, Sensitivity About Others; and Sensitivity About

One's Environment. Many people may experience some of these signs from time to time but a highly sensitive person will feel " too much" and "feel too deep." Some people might be highly sensitive to just one or two stimuli, while others may be strongly affected by more than one.

Sensitivity About Oneself

Sensitivity About Oneself refers to the difficulty of letting go of negative thoughts and emotions. When something unpleasant happens during the day they frequently feels physical symptoms such as stress or headache but often experiences tension or anxiety. Bad days affect eating and or sleeping habits in an unhealthy way, such as eating or sleeping too much or too little. When falling short of own expectations they tend to "beat oneself up". They are afraid of rejection, even in relatively minor situations. Often they compare themselves with others often (in physical, relational, social, work, financial, or other scenarios), wuth the result of feeling unhappy from negative social comparison. Most of the time they feel anger or resentment about situations in life or in society which seem annoying, unfair or aggravating.

Sensitivity About Others

The tendency to worries about what others are thinking or taking things personally. When triggered by relatively small unpleasantness with people highly sensitive people find difficult to just let it go. They feel hurt easily and frequently. They try hard to keep a lot of negative emotions inside in order to hide negative feelings, believing they are too strong, turbulent, embarrassing or vulnerable to share. First, Their life is like a drama so they discuss negative emotions with others. Every time they have a hard time accepting critical feedback, even when it's given reasonably and constructively. For that reason they often overreacts to real or perceived slights and provocations. Feeling awkward in group situations they prefer to stay alone. The constant need to feel the approval by others make them feel unreasonably afraid of being judged or rejected by partner.

Sensitivity About One's Environment

A kind of person who feels uncomfortable in a room full of people talking or in large public crowds when exposed to bright lights, loud sounds, or certain strong scents; a person who startles easily at sudden noises, fast traffic, or other unpleasant surprises and dislikes "shock" entertainment When watching or reading negative news in the media the highly sensitive person feels upset. It is also happen to feels disheartened when following people's posts on social media.

Furthermore to calm and alleviate overstimulation many highly sensitive people utilize emotional immunity and sensory immunity strategies to managing oversensitivity. For those who live or work with highly sensitive individuals, effective communication skills are a must to foster positive and constructive relationships.

HSP and SPS

Around 15 to 20 % of the population possess sensory-processing sensitivity (SPS). Biologists have discovered that more than 100 species of animals, including dogs, cats, horses, and even fruit flies, can possess sensory-processing sensitivity.

The terms HSP and SPS originated in the mid-1990s by research psychologist Elaine Aron, who theorized that it is an inherent trait an "innate survival strategy" so technically "observant before acting" and this help individual with more sensitive nervous systems better cope with the world by being   Other studies indicate that HSPs actually exhibit increased blood flow in the areas of the brain that process emotion, awareness, and empathy.Another common experience for HSPs: internally struggling with self-doubt and low esteem because you feel broken. Generally speaking, HSPs are more aware of and affected by external stimuli than non-HSPs.

High sensitivity is not a disorder but at the same time it is not equivalent of being introverted or shy. About 30% of HSPs are extroverts. They are often empaths, meaning they possess a keen ability to sense others' feelings, needs, and insecurities. HSPs have rich inner worlds that allow them to internalize everything more deeply from social interactions to emotions to physical and visual. The downside to these perceptive abilities is that HSPs can easily become overwhelmed. Criticism can not be easily digest even because not everyone communicates with the same thoughtfulness and tendency for nuance as HSPs. Because high sensitivity is widely misunderstood, the behavior of HSPs can confound and even frustrate others.

Most of the characteristic of HSP is:

- Master of emotional intelligence and relating to others;

- Vibrant inner life;

- You think before you act,

- Excellent strategy and planning yourself

- Consciousness and readyness, which makes you trustworthy and reliable.

- Prudence and problem solving-skill

- Sensitivity as high sensitive individual love connecting with other and get into deep, far-deep, far-ranging topics;

- Sensibility to the pain or suffering of other human

beings. This is why HSPs tend to excel in careers like medicine, teaching, and even social entrepreneurship.

Empathic

Emphatic is the ability to understand another person's reality while thinking about or being aware of their feelings. When a highly sensitive people listen carefully to their inner voice, amazing things can be done and brought to this world and the people around us. Feeling more than other people can be the source of creating the most beautiful things, having deep relationships, and being aware of the outside and inner world. Highly sensitive people tend to view and understand the world around them by using intuition and emotion. This causes them to be very empathetic in general. It is crucial to understand others, and a lack of empathy is what characterize those who will ever enrich our path, rather they just darken our path and make it difficult to go ahead. Without any interest in putting themselves in another person's shoes.

There are cases of disinterested people who lack empathy so this kind of people don't care about others don't have the ability or interest to understand or perceive how another person feels. They aren't sensitive, so it means that even if you tell them how you are thinking and feeling, they do not show interest in perceiving and understanding what you're going through. They are not worry about you maybe because they are too focused on themselves. Otherwise because they just don't care about what happens to you. They aren't compassionate so these people don't feel compelled to relieve other people's pain or suffering. Therefore, they're cold when talking to other people. It's hard for them to believe in others' feelings so they hardly feel safe with others people around. People who are disinterested in others' well-being doubt their emotions. With these characteristics in mind, it may be easier for you to see that those are people who lack empathy don't put themselves in another person's shoes. Therefore, they disregard others' feelings, thoughts, and desires.

One of the most outstanding characteristics in people who lack empathy is their selfishness. They think about their own well-being first without thinking about others' needs. Also, they take advantage of situations and people for their own benefit. In addition, they push the boundaries of reciprocity: they only give if they get something in return. They don't do things disinterestedly. They relate to us in almost a standoffish way, making manipulation a way of life.

When you address selfish people you probably end up feeling misunderstood or that they don't care about us. This is because they are only concerned about their own well-being. Being unfriendly it is difficult to be connected with others.

Some psychological disorders closely related to a lack of empathy are:

- Psychopathy: a disorder which is related to the inability to adapt to social norms. Psychopathic can not connect with others;

- Narcissistic personality disorder: refers to self-centered people who can't see beyond themselves so they only care about themselves. In addition, they leave others behind.

- Borderline personality disorder: People who suffer from BPD have emotional instability, which makes it difficult for them to maintain stable relationships. It is hard for them to understand and predict how others are feeling.

A person who lacks empathy can inflict a lot of pain on those who are very empathetic. Most of the time when you make an effort to explain to these people how their actions hurt you, they usually do not understand your explanation and will even try and make you feel guilty.

Additionally these people may try to manipulate you to get what they want. To deal with them you should set boundaries and decide how far these people can go with you, be careful when you choose your friends. Whether you feel that the people in your life don't make you a priority, leave them behind. Be as communicate as possible say what you want to say in the best way possible. If sometimes we can make the mistake of only seeing our interests this does not mean that you are not empathetic. They are controlling and cold so avoid these people who twist your thoughts to make you feel guilty. Feeling everything more intensely does not mean being weak. Being highly sensitive doesn't make a person weak, but it does mean HSPs have to manage themselves and their relationships, work, and lives differently than most people in order to thrive. It is a gift to feel strong, rather you are empowered because of happiness, joy, love, and hope can also be intensely felt. Many highly sensitive people are incredible creators. They use all those deep feelings of sadness, love, hope, anger, and happiness to create and they will often see the wonder and beauty in small things and have strong artistic sense. This could be in the form of music, poetry, art, dance, stories, pictures, etc. If you consider yourself a highly sensitive person, treasure it.

Stigma of Being Sensitive

Being sensitive is not seem in the same way in every culture. While in China a sensitive person is often most chosen by others to be friends or playmates, in Western societies considerate high sensitivity as a flaw. A high sensitive people is identified as someone who frequently feel deep emotions like crying and their need to retreat and recharge are seen as weaknesses, whether in the context of the workplace, romantic relationships, or beyond. As a result is too risky to tell other people what you really feel even when it comes to being open and honest about their sensitivity. It can be frustrating to be hyper-attuned to every minor criticism or conflict.

Contrary to popular belief, embracing high sensitivity qualities like deep self-awareness, emotional intelligence, stress management, and thoughtful communication are the hallmarks of healthy functioning and not signs that you lack the grit and competitive drive needed to succeeded.

Growing awareness is a trait that gradually move into the collective consciousness, allowing sensitive individuals to better understand themselves and communicate their differences to others.

High sensitivity is a double-edged sword. However, they need to shift their mindset to view their high sensitivity as a gift rather than a curse, despite cultural norms and naysayers who tell them otherwise.

Feeding Our Teeming Brain

USC professor Irving Biederman has investigated the neuroscience and affirms that the more a new piece of information tickles that part of your brain where you interpret the scene or conversation, the bigger the opioid hit. In fact in the areas of the cortex that initially receive visual or auditory information, opioids are sparse. On the other hand, in association areas where the sensory information triggers memory and taps into previous knowledge, there is a high density of opioid receptors. The things that you learn and are stored in one area can often be applied to others. Let's take Leonardo da Vinci, for instance, he was a genius by any reasonable standard, achieved competence across a diverse set of fields, including art, music, science, anatomy, engineering, architecture, and many others. By exposing himself to such a rich variety of input, da Vinci found patterns that others never noticed. This vastly amplified his problem-solving abilities. Even if somebody would argue that such wide-ranging interests were a result of his intelligence.

A clear-eyed analysis shows that "genius" is really a set of exceptional skills cultivated through disciplined study. One way to help genius to track ideas and stimulate more awareness of a wider range of disciplines is to utilize mind mapping or idea mapping. A simply task like searching the Web appears to enhance brain circuitry in older adults, demonstrating that our brains are sensitive and can continue to learn as we grow older.

How digital technology affects our brains

According to some studies daily exposure to high technology such as computers, smart phones, video games, search engines such as Google and Yahoo stimulates brain cell alteration and neurotransmitter release, gradually strengthening new neural pathways in our brains while weakening old ones. Exposure to technology alters brain circuitry, and young developing brains which usually have the greatest exposure are the most vulnerable.

Nowadays, video-game brain, Internet addiction, and other technology side effects appear to be suppressing frontal-lobe executive skills and our ability to communicate face-to-face. We are witnessing the beginning of a brain gap that separates digital natives, born into 24/7 technology, and digital immigrants, who came to computers and other digital technology as adults. This is our society today, a society in where our brains are developing circuitry for online social networking and are adapting to a new multitasking technology culture.

Intellectual Overexcitability (OEs)

Intellectual Overexcitability is defined as the processing information and decision making localized in the cognitive sphere. It is manifested as a drive to ask probing questions, quest for knowledge, theoretical thinking, reverence for logic, preoccupation with theoretical problems. Most frequently associated with exceptional abilities in children. High learning potential individual, especially those who display Intellectual Overexcitability, are highly curious and voracious in their pursuit of knowledge in their areas of interest, willing to occupy themselves independently and allowing parents to get on with their own work. These OEs are categorized as psychomotor, intellectual, imaginative, emotional and sensual, and many writers and educators use them as a basis for identifying gifted and talented individuals.

In particular, child with intellectual overexcitability needs support and more understanding. This will be a very valuable source of reassurance in this unsettling time. Parents should be very careful when it comes to understand your child's overexcitability by reading up and researching it, then you will be best placed to know how to support them and to show that you understand them. There is the possibility that this overexcitability will lead to a child devouring the schoolwork set by their teachers and an easy ride for parents. A child with intellectual overexcitability can not guarantees that their enthusiasm and voracity will be directed towards the national curriculum, and they may very well have their own ideas about what they want to research or learn. It is important to allow them the chance to really express their overexcitability. Being able to find a positive in such a strange situation will be important for their well-being and make the unsettling time much more bearable.

The stage of your child's education and the appropriateness of the level of work sent home may also be determining factors in any such decision. Either way, have confidence in what feels right for you and your child. If you need to discuss things with their teacher, then do so, every teacher understands that this is not a normal learning situation and that families have to work out the best way for them to balance the demands of work, school and also the well-being of the child in these strange and unnerving times.

Even the most independent-minded child with intellectual overexcitability may benefit from new ideas and the possibilities of new "place" to dive into, especially if unsettled by the current situation. Ideally, it would be great to find new resources in their area of interest or to provide ideas to mix it up a bit and try something new. It is true that in some cases there is an interest in the work set by school, albeit often with a desire to delve deeper. Therefore it may be that during these already trying times, there are battles raging across the country between parents trying to get their child to complete work set by their school and intellectually overexcitable children with their own, very different ideas about what they want to spend their time studying. Understand that this is a potential issue and keep an eye out for signs. A child with Intellectual Overexcitability is by no means immune to anxieties about the situation. Indeed, due to their asynchronous development, they may well have a heightened awareness of current events but not the emotional skills that would enable them to deal with it. Look out for anxiety, reassure them, and remember that, however high their cognitive ability, they are still children in an unsettling situation.

Chapter Eight

Enneagram origin

The Enneagram is a typology system that describes human personality as a number of interconnected personality types. The origins of the Enneagram are something of a mystery. It might date back to the time of the ancient Greeks, although its exact history is disputed. A philosopher and mystic by the name of George Ivanovich Gurdjieff is credited with bringing the Enneagram figure to the attention of the world, although he did not first use it to categorize personality types. He is the teacher of Inner Work who first presented the Enneagram to the West, made this dynamic the central feature of his teachings, and these terms have found their way into the mainstream study of the Enneagram of personality. It was Oscar Ichazo, the founder of a school for human potential and self-development, who assigned different personality types to each of the nine positions in the Enneagram diagram. Later, psychiatrist Claudio Naranjo expanded the theory to expand the nine types in psychological terms.

The Enneagram is the most powerful tool for developing awareness but it is truly effective only when we have a real and experiential understanding of relationship of Essence and Personality:

- Essence stands for what we are born with, prior to developing traits and psychological patterning. It is the part of us that feels most real, sensitive, and wise and is the true source of what makes us unique;

- The personality is the part of us that is functional and self-protective, the part that helps us organize our experience and to accomplish goals big or small. The personality develops around Essence as the sum of everything we learn and acquire through life experience.

In everyday conversation we often use the word "personality" to characterize what makes us special, what make us distinct and what accounts for how we perceive things in the way we do. However, personality is something more specific: Personality is the structured part of Essence, with a limited palette of actions, thoughts, and emotions. It's the psychological structure of our Enneagram Type, including the way that our temperamental and hereditary traits become crystallized into patterns, and the ways that these patterns continue to be reinforced through memories.

In Enneagram studies, the term "Personality" and "Ego" are often confused used interchangeably. When we believe we are the Personality, Essence goes unrecognized and unintegrated. Ego means "I am", and it's the sense that the personality and the psychological activity of the personality is "me". Essence is not functional. It simply "is" or in other words is the present.

Often our Personality has the expectation that "finding" Essence will be a kind of major spiritual revelation that when we have moments of connecting with Essence, we tend not to recognize those moments as such. Personality can't be present as it is based on memory and habit. It has no authentic volition and cannot make the personal, sensitive, and direct contact that is integral to the nature of Essence. Additionally, Essence in most people is so passive and weak that we become wholly identified with the Personality and forget our authentic nature. Personality is a kind of system for our basic Instinctual Drives shared by all animal life to attend to basic biological and emotional needs of survival, sexual attraction and of creating and sustaining relationships.

Ideally, our sense of identity, the feeling of "I", comes from Essence. Without working on ourselves our capacity to experience Essence diminishes and we become more fully fixated on the Personality. Our consciousness falls into automatic patterns based on recycled impressions from the past rather than a fresh engagement with the present. We suffer in this zombie-like condition even if we're not always aware of our suffering.

While Enneagram has become popular within spirituality and business disciplines, there has been limited research on its use and it is not widely accepted in the field of evidence-based psychology. It is a synthesis of a number of different spiritual traditions, including elements of Christianity, Judaism, Buddhism, and Hinduism.

Qualities of Essence

The Enneagram describes Nine facets. Each nine-point represents a personality type. The Enneagram figure or diagram is made up of three elements. The outer part is made up of a circle, which then contains a triangle and an irregular hexagon. These faces can be defined as interrelated ways in which Essence is differentiated and how these Nine facets of Essence can be covered over by identification with the Personality. Our Enneagram Type is not just a list of contrasting positive and negative traits, but a way of knowing the qualities of Essence most intimately associated with what's core to our true identity, and the negative behaviors and the suffering that result when we are disconnected from Essence.

Each of the nine personality types is characterized by a set of dominant behaviors, motivations, and fears. The aim is to better understand your type so that you will be able to make the most of your strengths and address your weaknesses in order to achieve your full potential. The Enneagram is often used within the field in businesses to help improve employee motivation and productivity. The employees gain a greater understanding of group dynamics and interpersonal communication.

Along with the basic nine personality types, the system grows much more complex and also includes 27 different subtypes as well as three key centers focused on action, feeling, and thinking.

Enneagram theory believe that people are born with a dominant personality type that can then be shaped by environmental factors and experiences. These two forces has the tendency to influence each other. Beside our innate characteristics our experiences, and the environment also plays a role in shaping how personality is formed and expressed.

The nine personality Types are:

- Reformer who is highly principled and tend to be perfectionist, purposeful, and self-controlled. These people has a strong sense of what is the "right" and "wrong" way to do things so they can be judgmental and uncompromising because for them nothing is worst that corruption;

- Helper individuals who are generous and people-pleasing. The have a strong desire to be loved, sometimes denying their own needs in order to make others happy. Sometimes genuine and with a tendency to puts a lot of energy into their relationships, but this is sometimes interpreted as neediness. Another quality is they are great listeners;

- Achiever individual who are successful, adaptable, and hardworking. Maybe sometimes they are overachievers or workaholics. They are focused on success than feelings, but are good at communicating;

- Individualist, people who are creative, forward-thinking, and highly expressive; they have a strong sense of identity so they sometimes seem self-centered but actually they are just temperamental or self-absorbed at times;

- Investigator people tend to be detached and unemotional; not only they are innovative and highly perceptive but also smart, logical and like to think deeply about things. As a consequences they are quiet, thoughtfulness as well as objective and logical;

- Loyalist, people who tend to be responsible and committed so they have devoted and trustworthylong-lasting relationships; their tendecy to worry so much or dwell on the negative can be something remarkable;

- Enthusiast, people who are spontaneous, fun-loving, and versatile. Highly extraverted because they are social and love to meet new people; their sense of adventurous is hight as well as the lookout for fun.

That why they are easily distracted and unfocused. Most of the time impulsive quick thinker but good at maintaining a positive attitude;

- Challenger people who are outspoken and action-oriented, They love dominating, and confrontational for that reason they are sometimes domineering, aggressive, decisive and self-confident. They aim at success in leadership roles;

- Peacemaker, who are greeable and easy-going they avoid conflict whenever possible because they can't bear disagreements; what they do is promoting harmony in groups, self-effacing and complacent at times. They even may ignore their own wants and needs just to ensure peace.

Sorting people into these nine different types is useful to give insight not only into the individual's own personality but also to provide valuable information on how to better relate to other people such as: Personal growth and development; interpersonal communication, team building, and leadership development; creating successful relationships at work and in other life areas. Furthermore, by gaining insight into individual strengths and weaknesses, people can look for ways to better relate and communicate with their partners.

Critics of Enneagram system

Some critics assume that the Enneagram system is rooted more in a semi-mystical ancient philosophy than in scientifically valid research and there is some evidence that it has a use as a personality tool.

In line with this, a study published in the Journal of Adult Development found out that all the participants who took part in an Enneagram training program showed improvements in ego development and personal growth.

On the other hand, one case study published in another journal, Contemporary Family Therapy, suggest us that the Enneagram could be a pretty useful tool in the context of counseling for helping to facilitate therapy and promote awareness in the counseling relationship. While promising, further research is still needed to explore the Enneagram's applicability and usefulness.

Tips for Using Enneagram Results

Since the Enneagram addresses faults and weaknesses as well as strengths in a person it is often thought of as a tool for self-analysis and self-improvement. This sort of test can be a way to gain insight into your own personality and might be a starting point for gaining greater personal insight and self-awareness but do not be only focused on results or take it too seriously. Everyone can work toward becoming more self-aware and achieving greater self-actualization. In doing so a few important things have to be taken into consideration. Discovering our personality is complex and a simple online test is not enough to tell you everything about your personality, behaviors, motivations strengths and weaknesses.

Despite the extremely popularity of the Enneagram, it has also been criticized for being pseudoscientific because it is often described as being overly vague and difficult to test scientifically. Some Enneagram theorists believe that personality is composed of a dominant type and one adjacent wing, while other theorists suggest that there are two wings. Besides, type descriptions have been criticized for being too general, and remember the Barnum-effect, a psychological phenomenon in which people rate personality descriptions as being highly accurate and individualized, even when they are so vague.

Whether the traits associated with each type are seen as a help or a hindrance depends on the individual and their culture. Enneagram area needs further research as it is not true that some type of Enneagram is better or more desirable than another.

The qualities of Essence

Knowing our Enneagram Type, we are in the good way to understand something of our Personality. Most of our strengths and weaknesses may be attributed to Personality. The Personality can lack development and maturity, and it becomes detrimental when we are identified with it to the exclusion of what's closest to our hearts.

The attempt to be powerful or gain power lead us to the forcefulness represented by point Eight.

Let's take a close look to the Enneagram qualities:

Power (point Eight): The full, vivid, and alive quality of our presence;

Harmony (point Nine): The direct recognition of the integrated, diverse and harmonized quality of presence;

Integrity (point One): The alignment with something greater than our individual experience.

Love (point Two): The quality of recognition that everything is cherished and cared for;

Value (point Three): Everyone and everything is inestimably precious;

Depth (point Four): The quality of presence that has indeterminate mystery;

Discovery (point Five): The clear perception of reality unfolding itself fresh;

Truth (point Six): The sense of presence as being fundamental and substantial;

Freedom (point Seven): Essence is not conditional by

anything, it is fully and completely free.

The yearning for Freedom comes to be searching for variety and a lack of contentment with the present represented by Type Seven. The traps of our Personality Type arise when we are unable to relax into the guidance of Essence. By practicing, we will be able to better learn to relax the activity of our Personality and drop into the Essence of who we are. Without connection to Essence, the Personality unconsciously attempts to manipulate our experience might feel like trying to simulate through activity or action what is only possible through the fabric of presence. We should better catch ourselves in the act of leaving ourselves, of becoming caught in an ego agenda, and learn to remain rooted in our authentic home, the Presence, while we prepare our food, pursue our interests, or spend time with loved ones.

Essence needs a healthy, strong, and adaptable Personality so that we can function, survive, and thrive. From this point, we can better understand that our spiritual practice is not to make our Personality better, but to integrate Essence and Personality more intimately.

Chapter Nine

Effective Communication Training

Not everyone thinks alike, talks alike, or is motivated in the same way. People differ widely in the way that they communicate, the way that they approach a task, and in their need for external structure or support. Successful communication requires self awareness, interpersonal skill and the recognition of different personal and cultural styles. Due to the rapport and effective working relationships with a diversity of people, staff members must develop the skill and flexibility to address the needs and concerns of different personality types. A powerful tool for understanding people in the workplace and creating successful strategies for effective communication and teamwork is, without any doubts, the Enneagram System of Personality Types. This is a psychological system which describes nine basic personality types, their point of view, their motivation and chief concerns, and their communication style.

Since everybody can improve their communication skills. The Enneagram represents a model of skill building and professional development for nine personality types while respecting individual differences. Instead of one size fits all, we can take the basic principles and practices of good communication and adapt them to each of the nine personality types. Everyone of us has an important perspective and contribution to bring to the workplace. The challenge is to get people of all styles and personality types working together well.

What you need to learn is:

- Recognize nine different communication styles in order to understand your own communication style and your impact on other people;

- Develop your communication strengths and overcome problem areas;

- Give and receive feedback in a way that works creating a rapport that avoid unnecessary conflict;

- Personal feedback and skill building and the ability to communicate in groups and teams;

- Managing conflict with different personality types.;

- Becoming a more effective manager, mentor, or coach;

- Guided interactions and roleplays;

- Forming successful, long term relationships at work.

- Using three centers of intelligence - head, heart, and body.

Type One: the Perfectionist

Speaking style: Precise, detail-oriented and with a critical thinking;

Strength: Fair-minded and authority based on personal integrity;

Common pitfalls: Overly critical.Sounding judgmental or righteous;

Meta-message: Recognize good intentions and hard work;

Their communication style demonstrate tolerance for other points of view. It is a good idea to give lots of appreciation not only criticism and mediate the quality of "rightness" in your tone and words.

Rapport with this personality type: and respect their code of manners take other people seriously. Do not forget to emphasize quality and share an interest in making things better. Avoid making promises that you can not keep.

Point Nine - the Mediator

- They can excel in their role of mediator, bringing together different opinions or different sides of an arguments. They can see value in most positions so

their communications may tend to be ambiguous.
However,.

- They seek harmony and comfort in their relationships.
  But they dislike conflict and anger, and hate being the
  bearer of bad news.

- They can feel threatened by new procedures or
  expectations for new behaviors. Rather than saying
  "no" to something, they will appear to agree but may
  resist or fail to cooperate fully.

- Once they agree with something or someone they can
  be enthusiastic and steady. They can be very
  convincing and persuasive from a deep sense of doing
  the right thing. As body based types they need time to
  process new information and find their own
  relationship to a decision;

- If they establish a position, they can be quite stubborn and resist change.

- They appear peaceful or unperturbed even when they are feeling resistant or overwhelmed.

Tips for communicating/relating with Nines

- To keep the peace, Mediator Nines can appear to agree, because they haven't said no. Silence does not necessary mean agreement;

- Establish common ground. Nines are likely to buy your agenda up-front to keep the peace and then feel trapped. If you want a true agreement, frame a conversation in which you state your own interests;

- Nines flourish with lots of support and value their contribution. However, they hate to promote themselves;

- Remember Nines like structure. When making changes, acknowledge the difficulties and ask for their cooperation. Keep the lid on sudden surprises they probably want defined procedures and clear lines of command. They definitely want rewards to be well defined;

- Try to communicate the overall context or the organizational need behind the orders because Nines can be stubborn about taking orders. If possible, reframe orders as suggestions in which the Nine has input.

- When you have to interrupt Nines do it in a friendly way when necessary, and ask for their help in getting to the point. Nines have a tendency to talk at length, sometimes avoiding the bottom line.

Three levels of learning with the Enneagram

Whereas the Enneagram is a complex psychological system which application does not depend on intensive study, Enneagram of Personality has the great advantage of flexibility since it can be used by people in business at different levels of interest and involvement. A simple workshop of one-day can offer important new learning that helps people become more effective in the workplace. With further study and practice, the Enneagram can serve as a road map for continued learning leading to increased professional success and personal mastery.

The model based on the work of Gregory Bateson, Peter Senge, and Chris Argyris, is useful for understanding how the Enneagram and other training programs help people develop because it utilizes Enneagram can be apply in three different ways with three levels of learning: incremental or single loop, reframing or double loop, and transformational or triple loop.

The first level: Incremental or single loop learning.

There is no need to be over enthusiastic about the Enneagram or understand the entire system. When people have identified their personal style, they have immediate access to a short list of specific suggestions that will empower them in the workplace. At this point one can focus on external behavior trying on new skills and behaviors. For instance, Perfectionists (Type One) can practice giving positive messages to balance their tendency to be critical. Speaking in this way is very effective. Performers (Type Three) can achieve better productivity by slowing down at times to listen to what other people have to say. Observers (Type Five) can make their knowledge and expertise more available by letting people know when and how to contact them and avoiding disturb them.

It does not take a lot of theory, or a lot of time, to provide clear directions for each type. Oppositely relying on teaching communication techniques or leadership skills in general, the Enneagram makes it very personal.

The second level: reframing or double loop learning

The process of understanding, and beginning to shift is called "Reframing" and it refers to one's habit of attention and point of view at the point at which the knowledge of the Enneagram starts to become internalized in the form of greater self awareness and self observation that people can carry with. Instead of behaving in the same old pattern, we have more flexibility and greater choice in how we respond. Simply, this means that in all kinds of situations, people are able to reflect and question their assumptions and reactions. We begin to see how our personal style impacts the people around us in both positive and negative ways.

In this case Protectors (Type Eight) can adapt to the situation at hand, sometimes stepping back to allow others to take the lead or observe their tendency to come on strong and assert themselves and decide when this is effective and when it is not. Having learn to set limits on moving toward others, Givers (Type Two) can achieve greater balance and staying power for the long run can notice their need to win the approval of other people by being empathetic and helpful.

The third level: transformational or triple loop learning.

At this point people are engaged in a process of personal transformation which means that they are willing to examine and change their deepest assumptions and habits and growth. Instead of avoiding feedback, they welcome it as a an opportunity to grow. They are now able to see that personality is no longer a bottleneck and they decide in a new light which is not based on a fixed position or identity. They decided by themselves to keep learning. Intellectual curiosity combined with emotional openness enable all the personality types to collaborate with others in the pursuit of a shared vision.

The ability to see ourselves and the events around us accurately and without distortion or bias is called personal mastery. The Enneagram provides the practical tools for individual awareness and professional development that make such personal mastery possible. When Mediators (Type Nine) can set priorities, tolerate conflict when necessary, and exert a style of grounded, fair minded leadership that brings people together for effective action are willing to step out of their comfort zone and let go of their attachment to harmony at all costs unleashing the higher potential of their type. Loyal Skeptics (Type Six) can develop their courage and ability to trust they have the capacity to inspire others. Having sharpened their perception and problem solving ability in large part as a solution to fear and doubt they will not use anymore their formidable intelligence to shoot things down, but they can create the strategies and visions that are the hallmark of enlightened leadership. They are now "encouraging" rather than "discouraging".

The Enneagram and Emotional Intelligence

The Enneagram is regarded by many business leaders and trainers as the most effective tool available today for developing emotional intelligence. Enneagram provides the necessary awareness and skills for developing greater emotional intelligence. For example:

- Other person's habit of emotion that is a key to their type structure.

- How they can increase our motivation and support others;

- How to best dealt with your patterns of reactivity and return to a more centered state;

- How to reduce conflict and find common ground amongst all personality types.

- How to increase your communication skills through rapport and empathy with other different personality, avoid taking things so personally.

Emotional intelligence (EQ) demostrate how collaboration with peers, supervisors, boss and so on is the vital ingredient to the success of groups and teams. EQ is more important than IQ whenever people work together towards a common goal including the capacity to know oneself, one's feelings and motivations, and the capacity to understand and relate well to co-workers and colleagues. Providing insight into how nine personality types think and feel, Enneagram supports our self knowledge and our ability to relate well to others, the two necessary aspects of EQ.

Margaret Wheatley in her book "Leadership and the New Science" reported that relationships evoke our potentiality. Everyone change as we meet different people or are in different circumstances. The basic building blocks of life are relationships, not individuals. Nothing exists on its own or has a final, fixed identity. All of us are bundles of potential. A report from Deloitte and Touche based on thousands of interviews indicates that only 25-30% of US workers feel that their best contributions are being harnessed. The shadow side of many organizations is the lack of "engagement" by employees. This means that the other 70% are either "disengaged" or "actively disengaged." The cost of this is estimated is higher and higher every year. By viewing people as living systems rather than static and unchanging, the Enneagram brings intelligence and resources to the professional development of individuals and their participation as team members. Every personality type has a particular contribution to make. The Enneagram teach us how to appreciate diversity. Each type has something important and unique to bring to work. Understanding the nine styles at work helps to engage each person's motivation to bring their full enthusiasm, their most brilliant thinking and creativity to achieving goals. In addition, it supports people to commit themselves to a process of constant challenge and development. The Enneagram supports not only individual learning but also organizational learning by assessing the human resources in any group.

Efficient and highly adaptable teams have the intelligence and flexibility to meet the challenge of this new era. But to be successful, managers and staff at all levels of the organization must be equipped with the skills that will make their goals and visions practical.

Defense mechanism

Some of the team competencies developed with the Enneagram are not only effective communication but also making good decisions, self management; holding the vision and getting results. Having good ideas and noble intentions are not enough. Whether efforts to restructure organizations and build teams succeed or fail depends on the ability of staff to communicate effectively and reach higher levels of cooperation and group intelligence.

Another reason for learning the nine personality types is to open up our ability to tolerate, appreciate and love people who are different from us. It is deniable that there is a lot to appreciate about each type, human diversity make us special. Contrarily, often the people who came in our lives can seem so difficult, frustrating and stuck in their patterns. Surely we become difficult and stuck ourselves. In fact it is the defense systems which lock us into our fixations and habits as it separate us from others from our true selves as well as separate us from unity. Self defenses is essential in our society and thanks to the Enneagram you know what you need to work on. Even if you do not easily disarm your defenses, a commitment to personal growth makes a huge difference. At first you are not able to change things as you might wish, but sending a signal to the authentic part of yourself and also to others, you will be able to understand you better and consequently your type structure avoid being completed controlled by the defense mechanism and keep your safe, or at least your ego intact.

℮ 162

Personality is the outer reflection of character structure. It's more changeable in different situations; character structure remains more constant although it can develop over the course of our lives. The Enneagram describes nine personality types but it is actually more correct to say nine character structures which refers more to how people are organized on the inside. It has to do with the building blocks of our psyche, the complex patterns and relationships between our many parts that enable us to function as coherent human beings. It also includes our sense of identity as we know ourselves. It is rigid in some ways, flexible in others. Its structure has the ring of consistency or permanence, but to call it your psychological "house" might make it seem more concrete than it is.

For most of human history people did not have the kind of personal boundaries that are necessary for an individual sense of self, at least not in the way we expect today. Distinguish between personality and character structure is a relatively new arrival on the scene of human culture. Human beings were not separate from the greater forces around them. Even the mythic Greek heroes on their quests were not fully individuated but rather subject to the control and caprice of the gods. The modern mental ego as we know it has taken a long time to separate from merged consciousness. As more complex personality has evolved, so also have the defenses. Our defenses are a key aspect of what holds us together for better and worse. In psychological terms, once we start dismantling our defenses we need to find new ways to hold ourselves to maintain a good "holding environment" with sufficient structure that do not make us fall apart.

It seems inevitable that it takes time to learn how to live in a more vulnerable state. Dropping our defenses is a painful and scary process since it brings up everything that we have been avoiding feeling or knowing. Yet there is a huge payoff if we can stay the course. We have more access to our true selves and we have the capacity for more love in our relationships. It is crucial that we appreciate ourselves for this courageous work all along the way. The Enneagram provides us with a map for each person's developmental journey. The possibility of knowing our type structure and our defenses (the idealization, avoidance and defense mechanism) allows us to distinguish between the necessary and positive aspects of our personality and our automatic patterns of reactivity. In this way we are more aware of how to apply good methods and practices. Today we have the benefit of ideas and techniques developed by modern psychology as well as the wisdom of spiritual teachings which are available to us.

Idealization pattern

Our defenses are organized into a cohesive system by three specific functions: the idealization pattern, the avoidance pattern and the defense mechanism. They are the cornerstones of each person's fixation and it is hard to think clearly or feel our true feelings when these parts are active. Working together in a three-way arrangement they keep the structure of the personality in place. You have to confront them time and time again in case you want to work on your personality. Although their purpose is to keep you safe, they stand in the way of our personal growth. The idealization pattern is about who you think you must be in order to have value and self worth. For example Sixes say "I am loyal" while Nines say "I am harmonious". In this way the defense system takes something real and genuine about you, a particular quality or aspiration, and turns it into a tyranny. This means that you invest your identity and your value as human beings in yourself. To the extent that you are attached to your idealization, to the point that you are not allowed to simply be yourself. Everything is judged and measured to some degree against this scale. There is constant pressure to live up to this expectation. Whether we fail in our efforts, it will bring up anxiety and feelings of unworthiness. You may think that there must be something very wrong with you. You think you have achieved your goal of being a certain way, but you are unable to see or feel things that do not fit this image. You can see this separation in other people when their actions do not reflect their stated intentions. Sometimes we can even notice it in our own behavior. On the other hand, if you succeed in keeping up the idealization, self-image gets put under the surface of awareness, and eventually the idealization becomes an illusion. At a deep level to put this even more strongly it is scary and threatening.

Avoidance pattern

The avoidance pattern works in symmetry with the idealization. They are opposite but they reinforce each other continuously: the idealization is supposed to protect us from what we want to avoid. What you avoid doesn't really go away but rather sits inside, out of view, where it exerts a big influence on your behavior and sooner or later exacerbate the very situation you want to avoid. However each type's idealization has a specific shadow side. There is a particular feeling state or experience that you would like to avoid, something that does not fit into your picture of who you are or how you should be. Put simply, if people want to feel "right" all the time there would be a danger that they will try to keep their "wrong" feelings and impulses out of sight. One of these feelings is anger. Nines become absent or stubbornly resistant, or sometimes they blow up when the pressure gets to be too much. Nines want to stay harmonious and avoid conflict, but conflict has a way of building up when it is not dealt with directly. Oppositely, Twos feel good about themselves to the degree that they can avoid their personal needs indirectly so for people around them, the neediness of Twos for attention and approval can be excruciatingly obvious. A Eight opt for staying strong and avoid their own vulnerability become emotionally isolated from others proving the point that they can only rely on themselves. Ignoring signals from my heart and body they will end up pushing themselves to the point of exhaustion and bringing on the very weakness or failure that they have tried to avoid.

Functionality of defense mechanism

The defense mechanism is the "enforcer". Try to image the of fierce guardian at the temple gates who jumps into action whenever the type structure is threatened, either by unacceptable feelings and impulses from inside oneself, or by something threatening from other people or the environment.

At different times, or in different conditions, we might find any one of them operating inside ourselves. But the Enneagram says that one of them is central for each of us the defense mechanism uses the strength of our type and diverts it. Threes use identification or role-playing precisely because they are so adaptable and good at promoting an image. Sevens rely on rationalization because they are so quick thinking and agile in their minds.

Defense mechanism, the last element of this system, supports the dichotomy between the idealization and the avoidance and keeps everything locked in place. It also can be seen as a chronic influence underlying the activities of our daily life. For the most part, the defense mechanism operates automatically and unconsciously. In the moments when you simply are not aware of what is going on. It does not necessary operates in response to specific threats to our personality, but at any given moment. Obviously, the defense mechanism will try to stop you from doing this. It is the nature of this mechanism that it operates without our making a conscious decision. It is automatic and and can not be handle easily on the spot. You often do not know until later that you have been taken over by it.

For instance, Fives may tend to isolate themselves and withdraw from a situation or person if they feel pressured or coerced as a general habit. Isolation from people, or isolation from their own emotional life, is a pervasive issue.

Usually is not the other person's personality type that is the problem. What really gets in the way of connection, cooperation or intimacy, is their defense system. These unconscious patterns are what create so much of the conflict and frustration in relationships. So whether this is anger, personal needs, failure, ordinariness, emptiness, rejection, suffering, vulnerability, or conflict, is necessary that you accept and move towards the painful and scary experience that you usually try to avoid. At first you have to fight a big confrontation with your idealization or self image. Over time with lots of self acceptance and support, you can reclaim the genuine quality within the idealization. In doing so, your self worth becomes more stable, your inner essence become more available to you, on a practical level you become more skillful in relationships, making decisions and living a healthier life.

Saying that you utilize a defense mechanism implies conscious intent, which is rarely the case. It is much more of an automatic pattern and it is very hard for you to see it in yourself. The first phrase involves the defense mechanism is "Ones use reaction formation" followed by the avoidance pattern and the idealization. Ones use reaction formation to avoid direct anger and stay in control of their feelings and instincts in order to maintain a self image of being right. The relentless demand of the inner critic to be good and do good at all times replaces personal needs and shuts down feelings. Reaction formation is related to the feeling one thing but expressing the opposite or at least something unrelated, such as feeling resentful but acting nice, feeling a need to rest but working harder.

Self-esteem depends on winning the approval of others. This can take the form of being overly nice, flattering people, and a superficial friendliness. It can also be considered as an attitude of entitlement. Twos use repression of personal needs and feelings in order to avoid being needy and to maintain a self image of being helpful. Repression is putting one's "unacceptable" feelings and impulses out of awareness by converting them into a more acceptable kind of emotional energy.

The pressure to keep up a winning image prevents access to personal feelings and needs. High level of attention goes to the external environment: the tasks to be done and the expectations of other people. Identification is stepping into a role so completely that Threes lose contact with who they are inside. In this way, Threes take advantages of identification to avoid failure and maintain a self image of being successful. Threes find it very difficult to drop either the role, or the image, since they get so much positive reinforcement in a society that values achievement and success.

Positive introjection is an attempt to overcome the feeling of deficiency by seeking value from an idealized experience, work or relationship and internalizing this through the emotional center. However this also leads to negative introjection. Their experience of loss or abandonment can take form inside as a self-rejecting voice which leads to pervasive feelings of unworthiness. Anyway, Fours like to use introjection to avoid ordinariness and maintain a self image of being authentic since they tend to blame themselves for whatever goes wrong in personal relationships.

Isolation can be physical withdrawal from others, as well as withdrawing on the inside from one's emotions and staying up in the head. Fives adopt isolation technique to avoid the experience of inner emptiness and maintain a self image of being knowledgeable. Acquiring knowledge becomes a way to create safety and self worth, but an over-emphasis on the intellect prevents Fives from connecting with the life force in their bodies and the support available in relationship with others.

Projection is a way of attributing to others what one can't accept in oneself, both positive and negative. While positive feelings are projected into a romantic relationship or an external authority figure to assure safety and justify loyalty, negative feelings are projected into others to justify internal feelings of fear and distrust. Sixes privilege projection in order to avoid rejection and to maintain a self image of being loyal. Sixes support their projections by finding and amplifying the information which fits their premise.

Rationalization is a way of staying in the head, explaining away or justifying things in order to distance from painful feelings and refuse to take responsibility for their behavior. Sevens use rationalization to avoid suffering and to maintain a good self image. As a consequence, everything can be re-framed towards the positive. Their ability to think of new options and possibilities allows Sevens to leave the present moment with its limitations and live in a seemingly unlimited future.

Vulnerable feelings are automatically put away and not experienced. What is reduced is emotional energy while instinctual energy is increased. Eights use denial to avoid vulnerability and to maintain a self image of being strong. Denial means to power up in the body center and forcefully re-direct energy and attention through willfulness and control. Since receptivity necessarily involves some vulnerability, Eights seek to impact the world and other people rather than be receptive to them.

Narcotization refers to be habit of using food and drink, entertainment, or simply repetitive patterns of thinking and doing to put oneself to sleep. Nines utilize this trick to avoid conflict and to five the image of being comfortable or harmonious. A life without conflict with others keeps Nines from being fully present in relationships. Even avoiding internal conflict leads to inertia and self-forgetting. Even productive activities can keep Nines narcotized if they become too habitual.

The isolation of Fives, the projection of Sixes, and the rationalization of Sevens shows up how thinking can create create distance from scary feelings and instinctual impulses. Energy is literally withdrawn from the two lower centers and concentrated in the mind in order to control one's internal experience and create safety through detachment. This style of reacting to fear is often associated with a paranoid/schizoid neurotic style.

Similarities and difference of Types

Both repression (Type Two) and denial (Type Eight) can lead to similar results in that both types become out of touch with deeper feelings and needs. Repression is a function of the emotional center and Twos convert them into other forms of emotional energy when they repress their unacceptable feelings and instincts. They might over-empathize with other people's feelings or they discharge their emotions through hysterical tone and affect.

Eights use the energy of the body center to override and close down unacceptable emotions. Emotional energy is diminished and bear down on their feelings of vulnerability or sadness with their angry forcefulness and obsessive control.

By contrast, the introjection of the Fours relies on using the emotional center and the empathy function to internalize positive feelings from an idealized experience or relationship while Sixes are looking for evidence for their position, holding an idea or mental construct about someone else while avoiding their own emotions and instincts. They try to see things that are really there but blow them out of proportion. Their emotional energy is amplified and they can overwhelm the mind and reduce their ability to think and sort things out properly.

From this perspective, Types Three, Six and Nine represent the three basic character structures using the energy of the different centers. The rest of us are variations on these themes, very different in external style and behavior, but related in terms of internal structure to our neighbors within these three center groups. The three centers of intelligence of the Enneagram maps construct a personality with a coherent strategy for survival and success in the world. You can make a connection to the world and other people establishing your identity and value through relationships or exploiting your mind to figure things out and create safety and options. Both character structure and defenses within the groups share a basic style reflecting our biological heritage as human beings. Body types are typically called "anger types" because anger is a main source of fuel for the type structure. Feeling types are also called "image types" with a layer of grief inside which results from the loss of self. and mental types are also known as "fear types" because this emotion is central to their experience in life.

Repression, identification, and introjection are operations of the emotional center. Feelings and emphatic connection are redirected in an attempt to earn external approval and create value in the eyes of others. But Types Two, Three and Four use their abundant emotional energy to avoid their defense mechanisms because their emotional energy often builds up and then spills out into the environment in somewhat ungrounded ways, these types are considered "hysterical" characters.

Each personality type has a specific defense mechanism which appropriates the energy of the lead center and uses it for self-protection. The natural rhythmicity of the belly center lends itself to these repeating patterns, which is why the body types are called "obsessive" characters. The body types all have defense mechanisms which depend upon concentrating and redirecting instinctual energy reducing in this way feelings and emotional expression not to mention mental perception. Denial for Eights, reaction formation for Ones, and narcotization for Nines are all forms of creating a defensive buffer or "screening out" operation which depends on repetitive patterns.

Mental types use the strength of the intellectual center not only to guide their decisions and actions but also to create their own style of defenses. A defensive barrier prevents us from knowing ourselves, our true feelings and needs. The work of personal development demands that you penetrate these layers of emotion and get underneath them to discover what is going on inside. Otherwise you simply bounce off them in all too familiar reactions.

Conclusion

Enneagram is an ancient spiritual road map that helps a person grow lighter and gain clarity once they have owned their lingering darkness and confusion. Enneagram is a system that can be used to learn more about yourself and people around you. Another reason for learning the nine personality types of Enneagram is to open up your ability to tolerate, appreciate and love people who are different from you. It is deniable that there is a lot to appreciate about each type, human diversity make us unique. Be aware of how you are is the first step to move forward and improving yourself in the best way ever.